Accidental Project Manager

GROUP

Accidental Project Manager: From Zero to Hero in 7 Days

ISBN-13: 978-1718792937
ISBN-10: 171879293X

Cover design by Luisito C. Pangilinan

For more information about copyright or purchase, contact:

PPC Group, LLC
439 W, Washington Avenue
Unit 405
Escondido, CA 92026 USA

https://ppcgroup.us
http://rayfrohnhoefer.com

In his latest book, *Accidental Project Manager*, Ray shares the story of Rhett Sero and weaves into each chapter the essence of what it's like to be an accidental project manager. It's written with a "quick start" method called "PROJECT" for accidental PMs to practice, learn, and put into immediate action. A must-read for any new project manager to learn how to move from *"Zero to Hero in 7 Days"*.

— **Naomi Caietti**
Author, Transform Your Leadership!
Managing Director, Naomi Caietti Consulting
Folsom, California

Those of us who actually started as "Accidental Project Managers" (but maybe slow to admit it) would have benefited from this this book when we ourselves made the transition from subject specialist to project manager. Much to be recommended.

— **Dr. Deasún Ó Conchúir CEng FIET FIEI PMP**
Project Consultant, Scatterwork
Switzerland

This book is a winning combination of valuable learning material combined in an organized and easy to read "story type" narrative. There is an intentional absence of jargon. But an abundance of good guiding principles for the "accidental project manager". I would have benefited from this book when I started out.

— **Murray Grooms, PMP**
BC, Canada

Highly recommended read, the style and the content are highly readable and should be very relatable for all functional managers being asked to work as Project Managers in addition to their 'normal work'. This book presents an easily usable framework to help you get results and increase your chances of efficient execution.

— **Deji Ishmael**
London, England and Lagos, Nigeria

Now that you have read this book, what are you waiting for? Start your P.R.O.J.E.C.T! This book contains best practices and easy-to-read advice that flows really well and applies to both new and expert project managers.

— **Nitin Kundeshwar**
Raleigh-Durham North Carolina

Accidental Project Manager aid's todays work force by supporting future opportunities in the field of project management without attending formal training. As a member of the armed forces this piques my interest and I believe that service members soon transferring out of the military could use this as a guide if they are hired as a project manager. The information included is a value-added connection for any service member by providing relative information, examples, and tips to aid them in the project manager journey.

— **Lance M. Oufnac**

A beautifully written book on Project Management which covers almost all the basic PM skills to help an accidental PM to deliver the successful project, this book can also be referred by an experienced PM as a refresher.

— **Pramit Kumar, PgMP, PMP**
Pune Area, India

About the Author

Ray Frohnhoefer is a passionate program management consultant, speaker, and educator with over forty years of experience managing software and technology projects, programs, and portfolios in multiple industries, including financial services and education.

Ray is also an instructor and faculty mentor at several Southern California learning institutions including California Southern University and UC San Diego Extension. His personal mission is to help individuals and organizations improve their practice of project and program management and many of his educational programs and consulting engagements focus on accidental and new project managers.

Ray's project management strengths include planning, development of innovative methodologies, conflict resolution, continuous improvement, and software implementation management.

Dedication

To my parents who encouraged a love of reading and writing at an early age.

To my fiancé who provided unconditional love and support for this project.

To my learners who always inspire me.

And to my muses, Hope and S'mores, for all the inspirational petting breaks.

—Ray W. Frohnhoefer

Table of Contents

List of Figures and Tables

Foreword

> "Stories constitute the single most powerful weapon in a leader's arsenal."
> Howard Gardner
> Professor, Harvard University

It was 1989. I was running to produce copies of the contract that we would sign that morning with a computer equipment supplier. After several sessions of hard negotiations, we had reached a win-win agreement. As I was about to finish, the CIO's assistant came to me, warmly greeted me, and asked me to come into the CIO's office when I finished.

Unfortunately, this reminded me when of my school days – I would get sent to the director's office when they felt I misbehaved. Internally I said to myself, "Please, not again!" as I headed to the unplanned meeting.

After a short conversation with the CIO to exchange pleasantries and our coffee preferences, he brought up an opportunity that was discussed by the board of directors. He mentioned the importance of gaining focus in our core business and the need to stop doing things that were outside of our substantive business.

At the end of his explanation he told me, "Jorge, we are very happy with your work and I need your help to conduct the Data Center Outsourcing project. I am sure it is a great opportunity for your career and I am confident that you are the right person."

I felt like everything was running in slow motion. I thought to myself "what in the … is outsourcing? What do you mean conducting a project? What is a project anyway?"

When I replied, "Su... sure, you know you can count on me," I didn't know two things. First, I became an accidental project manager. Second, I fell in love with this incredible discipline.

At that time of my career, I had never been in charge of a project. I didn't have a clue about what a project was and what kind of dynamics were in place within a project. Besides that, I had never ever heard a word like outsourcing. It was evident that I lacked the most basic qualifications to run the project, however I was assigned as project manager ... HOW DO YOU SAY NO TO THE CIO, right?

At the end, we finished the project within budget but late. I learned a lot: I learned what not to do, what to pay attention to, and the role of communications in managing a project. I also learned that the sponsor has a very important role to play in the project and if he's not connected to it, the project will suffer.

Fast forwarding to 2018 I had been in charge of several projects. In fact, I make my living by delivering projects to my customers. I studied project management. I joined and volunteered for the Project Management Institute (PMI) and attended all the conferences and classes that I could. Because of my infatuation with project management, I made a personal decision: To become the best project manager I could be.

Precisely when I was part of the board of PMI Mexico Chapter, I attended PMI's Leadership Institute's Meeting. I joined a presentation held by Ray Frohnhoefer who was speaking about ethics and the importance of having a succession plan in a PMI chapter board. Ray's presentation was indeed revealing and it was just what we needed for our Chapter. At the end of his conference, I approached him and exchanged some points of view. I was greatly surprised, that he was more than willing to share and guide me to our first steps into the succession plan of our chapter.

Years later, Ray and I had the chance to work together again in 2010 as team mates when we attended PMI's Leadership Institute Masters Class. I had the opportunity to get to know him better and I have to say that I have learned a lot from him. He has a true vocation to help others. We had good and long chats about project management, life as a volunteer, and we enjoyed and discussed endless hours about how can we help people to become better project managers and better human beings.

I wish that when I started my career in this field, there was a book like the one you have in your hands now. I am sure that the road would be less painful and more rewarding just by knowing the basics. However, like me, several thousands of practitioners around the world have been, or are about to become, accidental project managers.

This book offers a practical guide to those who are jumping from technical and other functions to the leadership responsibilities of a project. In my humble opinion, after reading several dozens of books about the discipline of project management, Ray has done an amazing job of synthetizing and structuring his more than thirty years of practical knowledge in managing all kinds of projects.

Using a story that depicts a very common scene in the day to day business environment, Ray makes us laugh, helps us to evoke situations that we may have thought were unique to us, and above all, helps us to understand project management concepts using mnemonic and other effective didactic approaches. Ray also took the time to include valuable references to information resources that technically support or complement the principles related in the story.

Finally, this book pays tribute to one of the oldest traditions of human beings - to tell stories to transfer knowledge. Several thousand years ago, our ancestors sat around the fire to share their stories, stories that relate their everyday experiences as well as a means to share their wilder dreams. This practice eventually carried us out to the stars, with an endless chain of projects as the platform.

I truly hope you enjoy this book as much as I did, but above all, I am sure that it will help you to advance from zero to hero real soon!

— **Jorge Valdés Garciatorres, PMP**
Ciudad de México
June 2018

Preface

It was the fall and the room was full of accidental project managers. I was teaching a State of California-approved Project Management Certificate Program class for San Diego Continuing Education when it hit me. I was talking about Earned Value Management (EVM) and I could see a room full of glazed eyes. This happened for a previous topic too, Activity on Node (AON) network diagrams.

Then I started thinking about my path to project management – it was the exact opposite of the path of an accidental project manager. I started by shadowing a project manager. I had access to training in both soft skills and technical skills. I started my journey prepared and learned a little more with each passing month and year. Learning happened at a steady pace, not from a fire hose.

I never paid attention to advanced topics like AON and EVM until I had to prepare for the PMP® Exam. Why? My employers' practices of project management did not include them and I did not find a need for them in my day-to-day toolkit, even as I moved from project manager to program manager to manager. That's when I came to the realization that my accidental project manager learners needed a book like this.

The *PMBOK® Guide* is now over 600 pages, addressing all project needs, including those well beyond the reach of the accidental project manager. It is not longer a "basic" book. Accidental project managers are already overloaded. Many are working on struggling projects or have just finished a struggling project when they decide to learn. But I was training them in areas way beyond what was needed or necessary at this point in their careers – they just wanted to keep their heads above water.

I looked at other institutions and found similar curricula. And more rooms full of glazed eyes. What could I provide that was far more basic, meaningful, and helpful than I was already providing? That was when I became serendipitously re-acquainted with Dr. John Estrella, a coach and mentor with a similar background and interests. John encouraged me to develop the PROJECT methodology and helped me establish a plan to "get the word out".

Rather than teach everything project management related, this book has distilled down the good and best practices to the bare essentials. I've intentionally left out much of the jargon and topics not needed for a first project. With a week of diligent reading and studying, the average accidental project manager should be able to get on the right path, with less stress for their current projects and no stress of learning advanced topics.

I hope you enjoy and learn from reading this book and have as much fun with your careers as the team and I have had in developing and writing this book. Like Rhett Sero, I encourage you to be positive and become the heroes of your projects.

— **Ray W. Frohnhoefer**
Escondido, California

Acknowledgement

There were so many people involved with this book that the best way to start is "I'm really sorry if I've left out your name".

First, I'd like to thank Dr. John Estrella. John is an awesome business coach and mentor – all of us who work with him have experienced awesome transformations for our businesses. Without John's guidance this book would probably not be written.

Next, I'd like to thank the many global professionals who have helped by reading, editing, and giving feedback and guidance for this book: Charles Adams, Sally Askman, Upendra Babu, Shweta Brahmakshatriya, Naomi Caietti, Carol Dekkers, Donna Eckstein, Jorge Valdes Garciatorres, Murray Grooms, Deji Ishmael, Pramit Jaishwal, Lori Kaid, Nitin Kundeshwar, Corinna Martinez, Deasún Ó Conchúir, Lance Oufnac, Theresa Pulvere, Naomi Caietti, and Jennifer Tharp. Your inputs and insights have been invaluable. Their insights have helped to ensure the material is appropriate for a global audience.

I'd also like to thank the staff at California Southern University and UC San Diego Extension for their encouragement and support of this project.

And finally, I'd like to thank the many folks that follow me on social media: Facebook (including Group PM360), LinkedIn, and Twitter. Your encouragement has shaped many of the book topics and in particular, the tips and "nuggets" that are included at the end of every chapter.

INTRODUCTION: BECOME A PROJECT HERO

What's an accidental project manager, you ask? Anyone who suddenly and unexpectedly finds themselves responsible for a project. Maybe the home remodel project turned out to be a little more difficult and complex than you expected. An organization you volunteer for may need a project to build a new wing for an orphanage and asks you to help. Or your manager gave you a project management text book and put you in charge of an important work project.

Congratulations, you just became an accidental project manager!

This book is the missing project management "quick start" guide for accidental project managers. What happens in the majority of cases is that accidental project managers fail at a project, and only then seek out training. Sometimes, if they are fortunate, they get the support of their employer. Usually they just don't know where to begin. Often the culture of their organization doesn't offer sufficient support.

Many also aren't sufficiently prepared to absorb all the knowledge of even a basic project management curriculum. Most could benefit from the information contained in this book – a quick set of basics they can learn in a short period of time to improve their early project experiences.

Accidental project managers come from all walks of life. They include employees with industry or subject matter expertise, those who may be in career transition, and transitioning military service members. They are also not specific to any particular culture – accidental project managers can be found in any geographical location where project managers are found.

Here's a brief profile of the typical accidental project manager:

- Mid-20s to mid-30s (and up)
- Develops expertise in their industry – works their way up the ranks
- Has little to no formal project management training
- Often receives little or no formal or informal organizational support for training, coaching, or mentoring
- Has good interpersonal skills, demonstrates leadership through work on projects as a team member, or owns their own business
- Starts with important, yet smaller to medium-sized projects with smaller teams – the work often isn't referred to as a project, however it has the hallmarks of a project

The best advice: embrace the accident! Perhaps the most important reason is that *someone is counting on you.* Your spouse doesn't want to live in an unfinished home for years. Your organization needs to control costs while advancing their mission. Your manager most likely selected you because there were no other candidates. So, clear your mind of those self-doubts – be positive and give it your best effort. You can do this!

Even the most seasoned professionals have been accidental project managers in some form or another at some points in our careers. Someone who receives training as a software project manager may know nothing about hiring and budgets when it is time to remodel their home basement – these may be project skills that aren't used due to the nature of the work projects they manage. If you have a knack for creating project templates and methodologies that teams want to use and executives want to see, you may find yourself promoted to a position in a Project Management Office. There you will work closely with project managers, supporting them with templates, training, and consulting. You aren't the first, and you won't be the last, accidental project manager.

Embrace your status as accidental project manager because this is your opportunity to explore exciting new career opportunities. Career opportunities such as these are not just where you are located now, but available globally. It is estimated that employers will need to fill 2.2 million project management and project management-related positions annually from now until 2027.

The career is financially rewarding as well – project manager compensation is 82% higher than non-project management roles on the average (Anderson Economic Group, 2017). There's never been a more exciting time to explore the career potential of project management.

Let's start by making sure you are really working on a project. A project is:

- A temporary set of activities with a distinct beginning and end date
- Activities which intend to produce a new and unique product, service, or other result

The project manager is often compared to an orchestra conductor. A project manager is someone who uses resources (people, equipment, and material), applies tools and skills, and orchestrates the resources to produce the project result. The project manager is familiar with the entire score and knows how each activity contributes to the final symphony.

A project is distinct from "operations" since it produces something new and unique, as opposed to making something repeatedly, perhaps with only small refinements or changes. Examples of projects include:

PROJECT VS. OPERATION

Project
- Unique Output
- Temporary
- Expends budget to produce result

Operation
- Ongoing and repetitive output
- More or less permanent
- Needs to be profitable

- Remodel a kitchen
- Design and build a new home
- Develop, market, and sell a new online course
- Create a new audio docent service for a museum
- Purchase and install new computer hardware systems
- Merge two or more entities after an acquisition

The fellow who claims he is managing seventy-two projects every week by mixing custom chemical reagents isn't really managing a project – he is repeating the same basic steps seventy-two times and earning a profit for his company. This is a process. If he decides he wants to increase his throughput to 100 shipments per week, that might need a project.

To help make the information more memorable, there is a process and an acronym that will help the accidental project manager remember the basic steps of projects. It's Ray's **PROJECT** method:

People
Requirements
Organize
Jell
Execute
Control
Transfer

The purpose of the PROJECT method is to get you started quickly, not make you an expert or teach you everything you need to know. To help deliver the messages, this book is written as a business fable. It follows the method as it is applied to a fictional, yet realistic organization and accidental project manager. This makes the character and the process more relatable and memorable to the reader.

Each chapter is devoted to a step of the method and ends with "Knowledge Nuggets" – tips, basic templates, and references for further reading and study. References include sections of the *PMBOK® Guide*, the Project Management Institute's standards for project management.

PMI standards are both flexible and non-prescriptive. They rely heavily on practitioners to interpret the standards and apply them to their specific project circumstances. What is captured in this book is the collective wisdom of "what works" for accidental project managers on their early project assignments.

To get started, please read the "backstory" of Rhett Sero, our accidental project manager and to-be hero. Follow Rhett as he prepares to manage his first project. Each chapter after this represents one of the seven days of his learning of the PROJECT method.

Backstory: Rhett Sero

Rhett Sero was a talented software developer for the Xanadu Partnership, a small San Diego software development company of about 100 employees. Rhett just finished architecting and writing the code for a software application for the Washington Corporation (WashCo).

Utilizing a Storage Area Network (SAN) device, he spent the better part of a year and a half developing a unique data warehousing application that enabled WashCo users to store millions of points of data about their clients and retrieve and display the data in a dashboard in near real time. Both his manager and the client were ecstatic with the result.

Rhett threw every ounce of his energy into the product – he loved his work. And when others on the development team got stuck and were unable to complete their work, he quietly and efficiently helped them to succeed. His passion for the work and leadership of the development team did not go unnoticed.

One Friday afternoon as his project was winding down, Rick, his manager summoned him to his office. "Rhett, I can't stress enough how thrilled WashCo and Xanadu are with your project results. Not only did you complete a project that exceeded customer expectations, you also demonstrated significant leadership through your work with your peers."

"Thank you, sir", Rhett replied sheepishly, "I really enjoyed the project."

"Rhett, your good work did not go unnoticed. Clark Inc. has been on our sales radar for the last six months. They want an application like the one you created for WashCo, however with many more features and expectations. We're estimating over 60% of the application will change: some big changes, some small, and all in ways you will be able to handle."

"I'm confident I can, sir," Rhett replied. "I just need a few more weeks to wrap up some details."

"Unfortunately, after they heard about your success," Rick continued, "we're unable to hold them off any longer. We need to start their project within two weeks from Monday and they expect that it will take no more than a year. You know the application better than anyone else, so we want you to manage this project."

"But sir," Rhett said with some hesitation, "I'm not really prepared to manage a project of this importance. I wouldn't know where to begin."

"That's OK, Rhett. Take the weekend to rest and give it some thought. On Monday morning, a project management consultant I hired for seven days will meet with you. She has a lot of project management knowledge and experience and is as passionate about it as you are about your software development work. I trust she will be able to get you started in seven days so you can help Clark Inc. achieve the same success as WashCo."

How could he rest? Rhett knew he had no clue as to how projects were managed – Rick simply told him what needed to be done and by when. He had very little insight since he enjoyed working heads-down on his code. He would hardly rest that weekend as he somewhat dreaded what Monday would bring. He never thought that he would end up being the hero of the story.

> **Chapter Pro Tip: Begin with the end in mind; pick the right method.**
>
> When managing a project, it's best to start thinking about the end goal and the steps you are going to take to reach it. Rick helped set Rhett up for success by quickly conveying the critical aspects of the project. As you will see, this plays an important role later. One of the first decisions that needs to be made is what kind of life cycle will be used.
>
> Predictive, also known as "waterfall", life cycles define the product as completely as possible up front and manage changes carefully. This helps to ensure deadlines and any contractual obligations can be met. If for any reason they cannot be met, there are usually early warning signs that enable choices to be made by the client.
>
> Predictive life cycles are best and most basic for the accidental project manager to encounter first. Since the Clark Inc. project has a stated deadline, it will be assumed that the predictive life cycle will be used.

PMBOK® Guide reading: Part I, Chapters 1-3 to learn more about projects and project management.

Article: The accidental project manager (Hunsberger 2011)

Blog Articles:
Plan projects like Albert Einstein (Frohnhoefer 2013)

You know you are a "knighted" project manager when …
(Frohnhoefer 2011)

CHAPTER 1

DAY 1: POWERED BY PEOPLE

As the weekend came to an end, Rhett could barely sleep. Sunday night he kept wondering about who he would meet and what he would learn. Monday morning Rhett arrived early, but apparently someone had arrived earlier. He found his white board divided into thirds. One the left, he saw:

---

4 Critical Tips to Succeed as an Accidental Project Manager
1. Clarify expectations
2. The importance of just enough planning: plan like Albert Einstein
3. Ask a lot of questions and think before asking
4. Give trust to get trust

On the right side he found:

<u>Projects Ultimately Succeed or Fail Because of People</u>
- People are impacted by the project
- People are involved in the project as team members
- Know these people – how they are impacted and how they work with the team.

And in the middle was an acrostic that spelled **PROJECT**:

People
Requirements
Organize
Jell with the Team
Execute
Control
Transfer

As he was pondering the source of the writing, a cheerful voice emerged behind him and interrupted his thoughts: "Projects," Mr. Sero, "are powered by people."

He turned around to notice that a slight, gray haired woman with a sparkle in her eye was standing in his doorway. She was dressed in a sharp and conservative business suit that almost looked like a military uniform. The generational difference was obvious, and he immediately wondered how this woman could teach him anything about project management for modern software development.

Without giving Rhett a chance to say anything, she continued, "Without the right people involved, your project will be delayed at best, fail at worst. A project I recently reviewed was delayed because someone impacted by the project wasn't consulted. They found a way to keep it from moving forward for six months. Do you know who the right people are for your project, Mr. Sero?"

Sheepishly he shook his head no, still wondering who this was and how she appeared in his doorway so quickly. "Maybe I really should pay attention," he thought to himself. He knew that Rick trusted this woman, so maybe he should as well.

"Good. Think first and always ask questions. I'm Miss Heldenmacher, young man, but you can call me Heda. I've been assigned to work with you and give you some project management tips and techniques. We're going to spend the next seven working days together and I'm going to make sure you succeed with the Clark Inc. project. I'm going to outline what I call the PROJECT method, one letter per day. We'll discuss the steps to take both before the project starts and when it is underway. I'll equip you with the basic tools to succeed. After that it's up to you. Are you willing to work with me?"

Rhett relaxed and held out his hand, "Nice to meet you, Heda. I look forward to learning from you."

"The PROJECT method is where we begin. It represents the basic steps you need to take as a project manager," Heda explained. "Before we do that, let's look at the four critical success tips."

Heda's success tips included four points:

1. Clarify expectations

    For this concept, Heda explained that Rhett really needed to know what was committed to for the project and what were the expectations of Rick (who was Rhett's manager and also the project sponsor), the client, and others. Through the

"Requirements" step in the PROJECT methodology, he would be able to develop that understanding and make sure his team did as well – everyone needs to be on the same page.

2. The importance of just enough planning

"What does it mean to plan like Albert Einstein?" Rhett inquired after a brief pause.

"Einstein said that if he had sixty minutes to solve a problem, he would spend fifty-five minutes defining and understanding the problem and five minutes solving it, replied Heda. "You need a similar approach with project planning – be sure you understand what needs to be done and plan the steps to get there before you start doing anything. While you won't necessarily have fifty-five out of every sixty project minutes to plan, the top project managers spend 91% more time planning than average project managers, and this is important to practice from the start." (Crowe 2006)

"It's equally important to be able to decide when you have enough planning," Heda continued. "Don't get stuck in what's known as 'analysis paralysis' – plans are useless unless they are put into action.

3. Ask a lot of questions

The third concept, Heda continued, "is to ask a lot of questions. Think first and use the facts at hand. There may be what are thought of as 'obvious' requirements, but do not make unfounded assumptions. Asking the right clarifying questions can save a project from failure. As they say, seek first to understand, then be understood."

4. Give trust to get trust

Heda explained that another important concept was that Rhett should give trust first to get trust. "Don't assume anyone has any ill intent – this will allow you to build trust faster," Heda counseled. "Team work is smoother if everyone trusts everyone else to do their part. We'll examine this concept more on the fourth day when we focus on team work."

Heda then moved to the right third of the white board, explaining that there are two main types of people involved in projects – those impacted by the project and those on the project team. She challenged Rhett to brainstorm a list – Clark Inc. management, Clark Inc. customers, Rick (his manager), WashCo management, and his peers not on the project team. Next, they started to identify who had the most interest and power. Sally, the Clark Inc. IT manager had both as this was her project – the rest of the Clark Inc. management team was somewhat divided, so had to be named individually, along with their roles. Very quickly the list was expanded to include more than a dozen groups and individual people.

Heda provided Rhett with a Stakeholder Register Template to document their findings, explaining that "stakeholder" was the term used to describe all the people impacted by or involved in a project. She asked him to think more about it overnight and then share with his project team later – together they would check to see if anyone was missing.

"It is always better to over identify, rather than under identify stakeholders," continued Heda. "One can always pare it down later. You will need to share the stakeholders with Rick, your manager. And for Rick and everyone you share it with, ask two questions: 'Who else should I speak to about this project?' and 'Have I missed any important stakeholders?'"

Once satisfied they had identified most of the people impacted by the project, Heda turned Rhett's attention to the project team.

She explained that the best people to work on the team are those who:

- wanted to be there
- had the skills to contribute to the project
- knew of others who could help.

Why are these three attributes important? Those that want to be there will show up every day ready to do their best work. And of course, it is important that they have the skills to do that work. Sometimes, the team may get "stuck" on difficult issues and that's where who the team knows can help. The team can reach out for solutions.

"Rhett, project managers, especially on their first project, don't always get to pick their project team. However, I'd like you to think carefully about who would be best for your team. I'm going to talk to Rick – while neither of us can make any promises, we want to hear your input."

"Communications is key," continued Heda, after they returned from lunch. "Project managers spend anywhere between 75-90% of their time communicating either formally or informally." (Haus 2016). She explained how Rhett and his team would need to figure out what needed to be communicated. There are four "must have" elements for facilitating project communications:

- Elevator pitch – a brief thirty-to-sixty second summary that describes the project objectives and its benefits. Use it to quickly relay information about the project to interested executives and others.

- Project deck – a compilation of all slides from previous presentations given on the project. Having the slide deck enables new presentations to be quickly assembled when

TOOLS FOR MESSAGING

1. Elevator Pitch: Short account of project and its value

2. Project Deck: Compilation of project slides

3. Status Report: Update on project progress

4. Communications Plan: What gets communicated to who, when, and by what method.

needed and increases consistency in communications and instills confidence in the project.

• Status report – this is one or more simple reports containing project status information, tailored to the stakeholder audience. Heda suggested that to start with, an overall status report would be delivered every Monday morning to Rick and the Clark Inc. IT manager to brief them on the project progress. Heda indicated they would look at this in more detail later.

• Communications plan – an often overlooked, yet valuable document that outlines what project information would be shared, with whom, by when, in what format, and at what frequency.

Heda provided Rhett with a second template: a project Communications Plan Template. She asked him to add the status reports and then work with the team and client later to determine what other key communications would be required.

"During World War II," Heda explained, "I worked with Captain Hopper. While she was excellent at getting what her team needed at the Pentagon, she angered some top brass. She didn't keep them well informed about the work of the team, she failed to report to some of them, and got others to work with her team without clearing it with anyone. There was no communications plan and as a result, people felt left out."

"As payback for the perceived exclusion, they purposely gave her team a computer without the capacity to run the software they knew her team had to write. It really impacted team morale and slowed them down at a critical time. Her team and colleagues confronted her and begged her to change and find better ways to communicate."

"While she developed her communications skills, her team invented virtual memory to solve the problem of the limited computer. It delayed their project work by months, but their virtual memory solution became the basis for most modern computers. By doing a little more planning and communicating, Captain Hopper and her team completely turned the situation around to everyone's delight. Xanadu and Clark Inc. are counting on you, Rhett, to have equal success."

As the day came ended, Heda summarized what they had covered that day:

- The PROJECT Method – P is for people
- The first step is to identify those impacted by the project
  - o Over identify, rather than under identify impacted stakeholders
  - o Consider the power and influence they will have on the project
  - o Ask who else will be impacted and who else should I speak with
- Pick the right project team
  - o May not always be possible
  - o Not just what they know, but who they know
- Project communications takes planning and people involved in the project need frequent communication
  - o Who needs information on the project
  - o The level of detail they need
  - o How frequently they need the information
  - o How the information should be delivered

Before he knew it, the day had come to an end. Rhett enjoyed the day with Heda. He realized how much he had learned about project management and felt better prepared to work with the people on his project. He looked forward to the second day with Heda.

Chapter Pro Tip: Over identify impacted people.

As Heda relates through her story at the beginning of the chapter, leaving a key stakeholder out of the plan may have consequences for your project. Stakeholders that are impacted may have an interest in, or power over your project. If left out, they may not care, but some may have hurt feelings, or worse yet, want to hurt your project.

Project professionals often use what's called a Power-Interest Grid to determine how to best manage stakeholders. The Power-Interest Grid divides stakeholders into four quadrants, based on what you and the team believe to be their power and interest levels. The quadrant the stakeholder belongs to informs the team how to best manage the stakeholder:

Low power-low interest: Monitor these stakeholders to make sure you correctly identified their level of power-interest and that their level does not change during the project.

Low power-high interest: Keep these stakeholders "in the loop". Make sure they receive the right messages, in the right format, at the right times for their group.

High power-low interest: Keep these stakeholders satisfied. Conduct periodic reviews or surveys, or other lower engagement means to determine satisfaction levels. Ignoring a high power, low interest individual may lead to sudden project issues as they use their power and influence to attempt to address their dissatisfaction.

High power-high interest: Keep these stakeholders actively engaged. They need to be consulted, given tasks, and periodically involved in some way in the project. They will be influencers in how work is done and can have large positive or negative impact on projects.

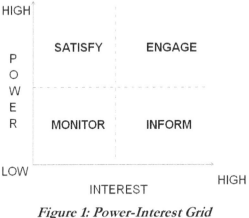

Figure 1: Power-Interest Grid

PMBOK® Guide reading: Part I, Chapter 13 to learn more about stakeholder management.

Article: Got stake? (Holder) management in your project (Forman & Discenza 2012)

Blog Article: Communicate, Communicate, Communicate (Frohnhoefer 2007)

Chapter Templates: Stakeholder Register, Communications Plan

CHAPTER 2

DAY 2: DIG FOR REQUIREMENTS

The next morning when Rhett arrived at his office, he found a big treasure map of what appeared to be Oak Island taped to his whiteboard. There was an "X" made with a marker and a dotted line connecting it to the words "Conference Room" written in a box on the white board. Rhett grabbed his coffee and laptop and headed to the conference room. He knew Heda would be waiting for him there.

After Heda quickly looked over the Stakeholder Register and Communications Plan Rhett worked on overnight, she nodded, and then moved on to the next topic.

"R is for Requirements," started Heda. "Requirements aren't something you simply collect or someone will hand to you – you need to dig for them like buried treasure. We call it 'elicitation' because we have to draw them out of stakeholders, just as you would have to dig buried treasure out of the ground."

"The first thing you need to do is plan your treasure hunt – a treasure map is worth a thousand words. Without the right requirements, you may not do the right project or deliver the products or services your customer needs. Or you may end up taking more time and money than was budgeted."

Heda continued to explain the importance of requirements for products and services and looking at the problem from all angles, technical and non-technical. She used another metaphor to explain the importance of good requirements: "I'm sure you've seen the movie Star Wars. What was the requirements issue with the Death Star?"

Rhett thought for a minute and realized that in the movie, the Death Star was virtually defenseless. "The Emperor focused so heavily on building a weapon of mass destruction that proper defenses were not considered - they were more of an after-thought."

Heda nodded in agreement. "The rebel attack caused damage, but a single, well-targeted shot was able to destroy the entire project in an instant. All the expenses of building the project were realized, and the value was lost in seconds."

"Poor requirements elicitation and requirements management is the number two cause of project failure," continued Heda. "In one survey, 37% of companies reported poor requirements as the cause of project failure." (Larson 2014)

"As the project manager for Clark Inc. and the architect for WashCo's project, you will be the one that needs to develop the requirements once the project begins," Heda explained. "You will need to start by asking some key questions:

- What is the problem to be solved?
- What information do we need?
- Who has or where can we find the information?
- What's the best way to get the information?
- What's the best order for getting the information?"

Putting together the answers to these questions will lead Rhett to a plan for understanding and writing the requirements and also help expose information he may need that he will not think of up front. He should compose a list of written questions to be answered to help the team understand the product they need to build.

These questions need to consider both technical and non-technical needs (for example, training and how the organization is formed) and look at all aspect of the organization. As he receives this information, it will provide clues for more information he may need. Time needs to be set aside in the plan to both determine the information required and then gather that information.

This is like figuring out the "x" on a treasure map. Critical requirements will point to where to dig for the next clue. Not every "x" will lead to treasure but knowing where to dig further definitely helps to better define essential project requirements.

"Now is a good time to review the Stakeholder Register, Rhett. The Stakeholder Register lists who has information and who knows where information is. There will be many subject matter experts, also known as SMEs that may be able to contribute to an understanding of the project. Don't forget to factor additional time in for this this important activity so that it is known ahead of time where you need to go for your information and insights."

For the last planning step, Rhett needs to determine if there should be a particular order in which he should collect the requirements information. Some of the order may be natural, such as getting high level information before getting into details (for example, you can't build a house if the foundation isn't ready). Critical components as defined by the sponsor should be worked on first. Some of the order may be dictated by availability of key stakeholders. Some of the ordering may simply be left up to Rhett's discretion. It is important to think through how each session to obtain requirements will be structured and ordered.

"Once your plan is in place, you'll know better where to dig," said Heda. "At a minimum, you should plan to meet with Rick, the project sponsor, Sally, the Clark Inc. IT manager who is the client, other Clark Inc. managers, and perhaps even some of their end users if Sally will arrange it. And don't forget to ask each of them who else you should talk to."

"There are three general techniques you will need to know to get the information: interviews, observation, and document reviews. You need to consider which is best for each piece of information and allocate time in your plan for these activities."

She further explained that during interviews, Rhett will meet with one or more people who have the information and start asking them the questions that will help him get the information he needs to successfully complete the project. She noted to be sure to run the meeting efficiently and effectively to make the best use of everyone's time. Here's another acronym to remember to have **GREAT** meetings:

Guided – you will lead and facilitate the meeting; set and meet goals
Right People – have the right people to answer your questions in the room
Effective – preplan the questions you will ask and be prepared to ask more
Agenda – send an agenda in advance; include key questions that might need preparation
Time-bound – respect the timing of the agenda; schedule a follow-up meeting if required

Each session should enable him to collect information to write **SMART** requirements:

Specific – provide as much detail as possible
Measureable –performance of the product containing the requirement must be measurable
Achievable –it is feasible to implement the requirement
Relevant – do we really need the requirement; should we do it?
Time-oriented – are there timing considerations for the implementation of the requirement

Consider these two descriptions of the same requirement:

1. The Automated Teller Machine (ATM) will dispense cash

2. The ATM will dispense cash:
   a. To validated and authenticated user with sufficient funds

i. in the specified account
ii. or in a linked account
iii. or by overdraft protection
b. Up to a maximum of $5,000 per day in $20 increments
c. Take under 2 minutes for the entire transaction

The second description satisfies the definition of SMART requirements – there are measurements and limits in place that can be validated and tested. If a two-minute limit is not achievable and the ATM will not operate within the specified parameters, new limits can be set or the project can be modified.

The person gathering and documenting requirements should document any assumptions and may have to consider additional information such as:

- How do we validate and authenticate users? Who are the users?
- What happens when the ATM runs out of cash or gets jammed?
- Does the ATM need to provide a receipt?
- If we link an account or use overdraft protection, do we need to charge a fee?
- Is there a fee because this is a network user and not a customer of our bank?
- Would customers prefer to select the bills or increments?

"There's never a guarantee that all the bases have been covered," Heda explained. "By being as specific as possible, the resulting product will have fewer gaps and issues and the product development team will have greater clarity. They may still have to ask questions, but they can focus on lower level details, rather than try to figure out the bigger picture."

"I think I understand," Rhett mused. "We had a team that didn't get the right product developed since they never really understood what the client was looking for. They asked lots of questions, but there were so many gaps that they got confused."

"Observation is another important way to gather information about how people will use a product or service," continued Heda. Since the project will be based on the work you did for WashCo, you should arrange to go to WashCo and watch how their users navigate the software. This may give him clues to things that need improvement for both clients, and reveal more about the requirements needed for Clark Inc."

"Similarly, it might be valuable to observe how Clark Inc. customers might use the product given they have a current process. Plan to spend some time watching the current processes, then ask follow-up questions to confirm your observations about what needs to be satisfied by the project. This will help you understand some of the non-technical issues such as the working styles of the users and the level of training that may be required."

"You should also review documentation," stated Heda.

"What documents should I look at?" Rhett inquired.

"For documentation review, gather any written user, business, process, and training documentation, documentation about the existing Clark Inc. process that will use or integrate with the dashboard software, and any other relevant information that might help with requirements elicitation. You may find clues to requirements by reading through these documents. Since this is a software project based on a current project, reading some of the code may also be valuable."

"Once you've reviewed the documentation, you may need to ask follow up questions that may have arisen during the documentation review."

Heda also suggested that for all requirements gathering efforts, it is important for Rhett to keep good notes. These should include who stated the requirement or where it was found, the level of importance placed on the requirement, and any other details that could be helpful later.

"At the end of each day worked on requirements, review your notes and determine if you need more information. See if you can put questions into future sessions to get the information or schedule follow-up meetings or calls."

Elicitation will typically have three common issues for which you need to plan to overcome:

1. ***Availability of people to participate in interviews or observation.*** Be flexible and schedule around the time of critical stakeholders. Also, be sure to consider if the information can be obtained from someone else who might have the information and is more available. For some information it might be acceptable to ask for written answers to the interview questions. If a time still cannot be scheduled, the project sponsor or client (in this case, Rick and Sally) should be consulted.

2. ***Conflicting information.*** It's very likely one stakeholder will say the product must be black and another will say white. This is an important finding because it sheds light on where there may be inconsistencies in definitions, priorities, and the understanding of business practices. In this case, see what other people think. No matter what, you will have to sit down with these people and talk it through. Building a model or prototype may be helpful - they can see what it actually looks like. In the event of an unresolved tie, a senior manager or the project sponsor may be

able to help with clarification or prioritization.

3. **Inadequate time.** Good requirements are important, but not perfect requirements. (Remember also that "analysis paralysis" delivers no results – action is required.) Some minor information can be filled in later. Of course, the best way to save time is to have a good plan and be sure each meeting is effective. Once again, the project sponsor should be able to help. In the worst case, just document where time ran out.

Requirements do not need to be perfect. In fact, getting perfect information comes at a high cost. So how will Rhett know when he has all the information he needs? Here are some of the signs – encountering more than one of these is usually a good sign that elicitation has collected enough information to write the requirements:

- A good working solution has been identified.
- Stakeholders begin to provide redundant information.
- A successful working prototype or model has been built.
- Stakeholders are slower to respond because they are unable to provide fresh information.
- The customer or project sponsor tells you they are reay to approve what has been completed.

"Rhett, once elicitation is completed, you will need to document the requirements. I'm going to give you a Requirements Planning template to use that will also help your planning process, and a Requirements Document Template that will aide documentation of requirements," Heda wrapped it up.

REQUIREMENTS

1. SMART – not perfect
2. Techniques
   - Interview
   - Observation
   - Documentation review
3. Common Issues
   - Availability
   - Conflicting information
   - Inadequate time
4. Elicitation End
   - Working solution
   - Redundant information, slow response
   - Successfully built
   - Customer or sponsor will approve

Rhett was thankful he didn't have a lot of work for the evening yet was ready to start jotting down some notes as the basis for his requirements plan.

As with the previous day, Heda told a story to reinforce the key points. "Bad requirements can lead to bad products, and bad products can lead to business failure," she started. "Three years ago, my local bank put in new Automated Teller Machines (ATMs) which accepted new credit cards with chips. These cards had to stay inserted in the machine for the transaction, not just swiped at the beginning. Whoever developed the requirements for the ATM obviously forgot about human behavior."

"People were leaving their cards behind. Many were used to just grabbing the cash and driving away, assuming the transaction was complete. For several months, customers complained to the bank because they had to take someone else's chip-enabled card out of the machine before initiating their own transaction. Fortunately, most people took the time to stop to return the cards to the bank manager."

"Within six months, the first version of the ATMs needed extensive modifications. The new software required that the card be taken out before the machine would dispense the cash or receipts. The solution required both hardware and software changes. It was an expensive lesson for the vendor, but when they looked at the problem from all angles, they succeeded."

And once again, Heda summed up what they had covered on Day 2:

- R is for Requirements
- Requirements need a plan
  - Information needed
  - Where the information can be found or who has it
  - Best way to get the information and the order to get it in
- Three elicitation methods
  - Interviews
  - Observations
  - Document Reviews
- Three common elicitation problems
  - Availability
  - Inadequate Time
  - Conflicting Information
- Some ways to know when elicitation has enough information
  - A good working solution has been identified or a prototype built
  - Stakeholders begin to provide redundant information or are slow to respond
  - The customer or project sponsor tells you they are ready to approve what has been completed.

ACROSTIC ACRONYMS

PROJECT
Method

SMART
Requirements

GREAT
Meetings

33

Chapter Pro Tip: Interview the project sponsor and ask "What does success look like to you?"

One great way to start elicitation is to meet with the project sponsor or client first and ask, "What does success look like to you?"

Getting the right requirements is not an easy task. And as you will see later in this book, project management also involves making appropriate trade-offs in scope, time, budget, quality, and resources.

This open-ended question will help you get to what the sponsor values the most in the project which will inform future trade-offs and decisions. The input will also provide you with a valuable starting point for requirements – a high-level vision for what the finished project will provide and what the expected benefits will be.

A common problem with some projects is that they produce a product or service that meets all the requirements, but the benefits aren't realized. It is important to understand the expected benefits to refine your requirements.

Some other good questions include:

- What are your biggest challenges and opportunities?
- What are some quick wins you'd like to achieve?
- What happens if we don't change or succeed?
- Who will be impacted the most and why?
- Who else will be impacted?
- Who else should I speak with?
- What else will impact the project?

> Asking these open-ended questions can evoke valuable information.

PMBOK® Guide reading: Part I, Chapter 5.2 to learn more about requirements. This section will refer you to another PMI publication which has more information about requirements elicitation and management.

Article: Requirements Management Made Easy (Davis & Zweig 2000)

Book: Unearthing Business Requirements (Hossenlopp & Hass 2008)

Chapter Templates: Requirements Planning, Requirements Document

CHAPTER 3

DAY 3: ORGANIZE OBJECTIVES

It was Wednesday, and Brett was already feeling more confident that he could manage the project. When he arrived at the office, Heda was waiting for him in the conference room. On the white board she had written:

A man, a plan, a canal, Panama.

"Heda," Rhett started softly, "here at Xanadu the programmers generally work up their own plans and give the dates to the project manager. Is there something different we have to do?"

"Rhett, more than just a palindrome, the expression on the board tells a long story of a project that originally didn't have a good plan," Heda explained.

"After France succeeded with the construction of the Suez Canal, they were eager to repeat the project across Central America. Rather than do a complete plan, they did one or two site visits during the best weather times in 1881 and ordered digging to begin. Mudslides, snakes, venomous spiders, yellow fever, and malaria were claiming over 200 deaths per month – these issues were not a concern for the earlier project. In addition, the same heavy digging equipment used in the Suez Canal project simply rusted in the always damp jungle. The project ended in failure and was abandoned for more than twenty years." (Panama Canal 2018)

"While it's a good idea to involve the team in the planning, what's been done at Xanadu in the past isn't really a plan. Rick tells me many Xanadu projects run over time and over budget. And while your WashCo project was a success, not all clients have been as delighted."

"Let's show everyone how it's really done and complete a plan for Clark Inc. that you and your team can actually meet or exceed. I'm confident you can do it," said Heda supportively.

"Today, we're going to cover the real planning work you will have to do with your team for the project," Heda continued. "O is for organize."

"You and your team will identify and estimate all the work that needs to be done, consider any constraints and risks that might add or subtract from your plan, and develop a milestone plan which will guide the day-to-day work of the project."

"Your project kickoff meeting and requirements efforts will be early items in your plan. Next you and the team will use the requirements to create objectives for scope (what the project will actually deliver) and the timeframe in which it will be delivered. Quality is normally an objective too. We already know Clark Inc. wants high quality and we'll see what else they add in the requirements."

"Since all the hardware is already in place and you are using only Xanadu programmers, you won't have to be concerned with a budget. Project managers, especially new project managers, rarely get to set their own budget anyway. Then we will organize all the plans and documentation to get the project underway."

"The first step after requirements will be to take what you know about the stakeholders and requirements to the team and ask them to help create a Work Breakdown Structure."

Heda continued to instruct Rhett on how a Work Breakdown Structure (WBS) is created. She used a recipe as a metaphor for a WBS. The name of the project is what is being made; the ingredients are the various components, subcomponents, and smaller pieces of work that will be delivered. The final plan will be the instructional part of the recipe, indicating who does what and when they will do it.

"In terms of the WBS," Heda continued, "the lowest level contains work packages – work that must be completed to finish the project. You can set up the highest levels; then you will need to work with your team to break it down into smaller pieces."

"Once your team understands what work is associated with each level and can reasonably estimate what it will take to implement it, they can stop breaking it down. Each work package should represent roughly two to four weeks of work and will also serve as a high-level design."

"Another important point is not to worry about how the work is sequenced at this time. It's more important to get the ingredients list solid first before going on to how the work will be done. Worrying about how the work will be done will only be a distraction. One of the biggest problems with not following this rule is that someone forgets a major piece of work that needs to be done and discovers it in the middle of the project."

Here's what Heda drew on the white board to show Rhett the start of the WBS:

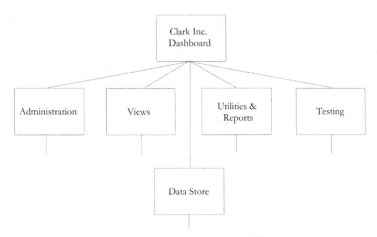

Figure 2: High-Level WBS

"The WBS should be accompanied by a WBS dictionary that gives more information about each work package," Heda continued. "As before, I'll provide you with a template. One of the most important things to include in the WBS dictionary is the acceptance criteria which will tell you that the work package is complete and of acceptable quality."

"For your software project, this may mean that the code has been unit tested by the developer and properly integrates with another module. Or that a module like a random number generator is actually generating random numbers reliably. Or that a sort is not only sorting but is also completing the algorithm in the time required."

"Once the WBS is complete, the work packages must be estimated for the necessary human resources and time to complete. These will become a part of the WBS dictionary as well."

In just a part of a day, it's not feasible to learn how to effectively create network diagrams and schedules using tools like Microsoft® Project®. So Heda suggested that Rhett should set up a Milestone Plan and present it to Rick and the client (Andersen 2006). If a more detailed plan is needed, Rick and Sally at Clark Inc. had agreed to allocate a scheduling expert to work with Rhett and the team to complete a Gantt chart.

GANTT CHART

A Gantt Chart, named for its inventor, Henri Gantt, is simply a bar chart showing project activities over time, along with their dependencies. Gantt charts are frequently created by scheduling software applications.

A milestone plan shows when the major components of the software will be completed, along with some of the basic actions needed to get there, such as the developers writing modules that became a part of a larger system. The plan should include at least one item to be delivered every one to two weeks.

To establish the Milestone Plan, Rhett will meet with the team to establish the design and together they will order the tasks. It will give the team an opportunity to determine what pieces of the system had to be completed for other pieces to work. Some of the work could go on in parallel, but at some point, all the major components would have to be integrated and tested together.

Once the design is complete, Rhett will assign team members who will write the code modules. Each developer will estimate how long it will take them to complete the work and more importantly, commit to a date when they would finish.

Rhett will first help them understand how many hours it will take them to write the code if they were not interrupted. This is referred to as "effort". Factoring in non-working time such as weekends, days off, and training days will get them to their milestones or "duration". As Heda explained, by having the team participate in setting the milestones, there will be a deeper level of commitment and the team would buy-in to the plan.

"What happens if someone is writing new code for the first time and doesn't feel comfortable making an estimate?" Rhett inquired. Heda explained he had some options, including:

MILESTONE PLAN

A milestone plan contains:
- Major project activities
- Who performs and by when
- Listed in delivery date order

- Share with the programmer historical estimates from a project with similar work
- Ask the team if anyone had done similar work or knows someone who has and can help with the estimate
- Ask programmers in his professional network if they would help
- Determine an average time if multiple estimate were available
- And worst case, use the best professional judgement possible

42

Since he was already an expert in the system, Rhett would be able to work with any member of the team who is not able to meet an important date, such as when the dashboard must be finished or when a piece of code is critical for another one to work. He will be able to use information from his previous project to make sure all the estimated milestones were reasonable.

Rhett's expertise and use of past and present estimates will help make sure everything completes on time. And if he feels that the project end date is ever in jeopardy, Heda advised that he will have to take the issue to Rick and Sally to get further help. Once all the information is together, Rhett will complete a draft of the Milestone Plan Template.

"Looking ahead to the future, when your team starts working on the project," continued Heda, "you need to understand that your project is subject to some constraints. The normal constraints are considered to be time, cost, and quality – they contribute to constraining the scope of the project. Your project won't be concerned with cost; however, you will need to consider the others."

"If constraints change for any reason, you will have to consider what else will change. For example, if a programmer needs more time to finish work, either the project will slip or you will have to find another resource to help. Or perhaps identify something that will be out of scope now and finished in a future phase."

"Likewise, if some code proves to be of poor quality, it may require additional time to complete. We'll look at the ideas of managing constraints due to change further in a few days when we look at control."

Heda continued to explain that another important constraint on projects is resources. If a team member is sick for a week, Rhett

RISK TERMS

will need a to consider how to best fill the gap and what the overall impact on the plan might be. Xanadu also had many other projects in progress, so it might be possible that one of the programmers has to work on another project for a period of time.

> Two main components:
> - Likelihood
> - Impact
>
> Risks with negative impacts are *threats*; with positive impacts are *opportunities*.
>
> Risks that have already occurred are *issues*.

"Overall, many of these things that can happen to your project are considered risks," Heda explained. "Risks can be further broken down into threats and opportunities. Threats have negative consequences on your project. Opportunities can have a positive impact. An example of an opportunity for your project is finding some reusable code that could reduce the work for a part of the software and enable you to complete the project sooner."

"You should work with the team to identify the basic threats and opportunities. their likelihood of happening, and the impact if they do happen. Most of them will be related to resources and time commitments but be sure to think out of the box. For example, what would happen if a pipe were to burst in this building and the team couldn't come to work? While everyone might be able to work from a laptop at home, would they really be able to work at the same pace and level of productivity?"

"Opportunities can sometimes be difficult to think of," continued Heda. "Once you start thinking of all the bad things that can happen, you will find your mind focused on that. One easy way to change the focus is to have two meetings separated by a period of time. I always challenge my teams to have at least 20% of the risk list be opportunities."

"The highest priority threats should have contingency or mitigation plans. A contingency plan is like a workaround – you will not eliminate the threat, but you will lessen the impact."

"Mitigation plans are changes you will make to your milestone plan and other plans to reduce the probability and/or impact of the risk. Before you finalize your milestone plan, the team should consider if any days need to be added or subtracted from the plan or other plan changes need to be made to accommodate threat mitigation plans."

"In a similar manner, you may need to modify plans or have workarounds in place to embrace and take advantage of opportunities. You also want to make sure that the advantage of an opportunity isn't negated by a longer plan needed to act on it."

As usual, Heda had a Risk Analysis Template available for Rhett to use with the team. Once the team completed the template and made any adjustments to the Milestone Plan to accommodate constraints and risks, Rhett will provide all the documentation – the WBS, Milestone Plan, and Risk Assessment to Rick and Sally for review. If the team did a thorough job, it was very likely that Rick and Sally will also buy-in to their plan and their reviewed and approved plan would become the action plan for the team.

"Rhett, if you follow these basic principles, you will succeed," encouraged Heda. Rhett could tell Heda was ready for a story so didn't interrupt.

"My very first project used these principles. We spent roughly three months in planning and five months writing the code, then three months to test and roll out the system. During planning we broke down the work, made our estimates, and put together an initial plan. Then we had some discussion about risks. We realized that what we were about to do was considered contrary to programming practices at the time, but that in doing so, we would create a superior, more maintainable system that would outperform existing systems."

"How did you handle that threat?" Rhett inquired.

"As part of our risk assessment work, we wrote and tested some small subroutines and captured their timing to demonstrate that our principles would work. Inevitably we heard 'that's not going to work', but we were prepared to show otherwise without wasting project time in a political battle."

"We also found an opportunity in the form of some reusable code that cut down our project time considerably. Our system remained in use for well over a dozen years and we accomplished in a year what our competitor took four or more years to accomplish with more resources."

Rhett had absorbed a lot of information about organizing and planning the project and was still confident he would be able to work with his team and succeed. Before departing for the day, Heda summed up what they had covered on Day 3:

- O is for Organize Objectives
- Planning is an essential team activity
  - First, create a Work Breakdown Structure
  - It's a lot like a project ingredients list
  - Don't worry about order now
  - Done when tasks can be estimated
  - Full information in WBS dictionary
- Each WBS work package needs to be estimated for resources and time
  - Top down and bottom up
  - Estimate effort first – convert to duration
  - Use multiple techniques to validate
- Consider constraints – especially time and resources
- Consider risks
  - Identify and prioritize threats and opportunities
  - Develop contingencies and mitigations
  - Monitor and correct as needed
- Document the milestone plan and get customer and management buy-in
  - Major project activities
  - Who performs what and by when
  - Listed in delivery date order

Chapter Pro Tip: Risk is like an iceberg ... don't be the Titanic.

Despite decades of research and continuous improvement, project failure rates are still unacceptably high. By some accounts and surveys, up to 20% of projects still fail outright and double-digit percentages are challenged in one or more ways.

Some of these failures are attributable to poor risk management. The oft cited reason for glossing over proper risk management includes insufficient time and a firm belief by many in project invulnerability.

The builders of the Titanic thought the ship to be invulnerable as well. So much so, that when they hit an iceberg, they lost precious time to save the ship in their steadfast belief that nothing could happen.

An hour or more later, when the ship had already taken on a lot of water, they decided to act – too little too late. And their earlier hubris meant there were insufficient life boats on board to save everyone.

The lesson to be learned is that having proper risk assessment scaled to the size of the project is not very time consuming. Most small to medium sized projects can complete a substantial risk assessment in under a day. Technically, it is proper to repeat the process any time there is a change to the project, yet once again, a periodic re-assessment may be sufficient for many projects.

By ignoring risks, problems and issues can be compounded over time. Risk management can be seamlessly integrated into project management processes and practices, rather than something to separately invoke in a time of crisis.

What's more, there is a positive side of risk – opportunity. By seeking opportunities, we can find ways to conduct our projects more efficiently and effectively, saving time and cost. So, in skipping risk assessment, you miss finding beneficial opportunities.

And finally, in addition to working within the project life cycle, the same process developed for your projects can be used to assess business risks, organizational financial risks, operational planning, and risks associated with operations such as manufacturing and supply chain.

And one more benefit … it is impossible to identify all the risks you may encounter. Going through the process of identifying threats and opportunities and their contingency plans and mitigation strategies will better prepare you for the time when the unknown risk happens. Chances are you have indirectly identified a strategy or are close to having a strategy to handle the unknown risk.

PMBOK® Guide reading: Part I, Chapter 5.4 to learn more about the WBS. Chapter 6 on creating schedules is a little more advanced, so you might want to re-visit it in the future. Chapter 6.4 covers estimation. Chapter 11 covers risk management.

Article: Milestone Planning—A Different Planning Approach (Andersen 2006)

Books:
Risk Assessment Framework (Frohnhoefer 2017a)

Risk Assessment Framework Implementation Guide (Frohnhoefer 2017b)

Chapter Templates: WBS Dictionary, Milestone Plan, Risk Analysis

Day 4: Jell with the Team

On the beginning of the fourth day when he arrived at the office, Rhett found another message on his white board:

Together
Everyone
Achieves
More

And underneath it was written:

Breakfast? Meet me at the coffee shop on the corner.

Rhett knew today was going to be about teamwork but wondered about the new meeting venue as he hurried out the door and down the block. As usual, Heda was waiting, this time with a hot breakfast sandwich on a bagel and his favorite latte. This little reward for Rhett's diligent learning was her way of reinforcing the lesson before it started.

"Good morning, Rhett," Heda began. "Remember during our first day together that I mentioned people make or break projects? The team is one very important group and you are going to have to be able to work with them quickly and effectively."

"Communications and teamwork are critical to every project. We're going to start building your awareness of teamwork today and will provide you with some additional skills during the course of the next few days."

"J is for Jell with the team," Heda continued. "The project manager and the team need to work closely together to achieve the desired results."

Heda went on to give an example of failed teamwork. During the 1970s she worked on a project to produce a sophisticated supercomputer. To speed up development work, the hardware and software were developed in parallel. Unfortunately, there wasn't a lot of communications between the two teams.

When the first integration test was conducted, it was found that the hardware design had the bits numbered from right-to-left and the software team had numbered them from left-to-right. This caused an enormous amount of rework and significantly delayed the project. When combined with other factors, the project was delayed sufficiently for a competitor to beat them to the sales. The project failed and this led to overall failure of the company.

"You've probably heard" Heda continued, "that teams go through development stages – forming, storming, norming, performing, and closing. With the edge of getting to influence who is on your team, having had an opportunity to work with your team on earlier projects, and your own development as a project manager and team leader, we're all hoping the 'storming' part will be minimized. Good teamwork and your management of the team will be essential."

Trust is what makes teams work well. As Heda had instructed on the first day, Rhett had to learn to give trust first, in order to get trust. Through leading by example, Rhett would be able to quickly build an environment of trust. It would initially be fragile, but he could take other steps over time to ensure the team worked well together.

"Rhett, you will need to spend some time at the start of the project getting to know the team more personally. Some of them you may know and have worked with, some will be people with whom you are not acquainted."

Rhett will have to work with the team to continue to build trust and everyone on the team will need to get to know each other better. Heda suggested one way to encourage the process would be to do some icebreaking and team building exercises at the start of all major team meetings.

"One exercise I found to be very effective is to ask the team to write about their 'dream trip'," explained Heda. "Ask them to imagine that the project is over and as a reward for a job well done, that they are given one month and an unlimited budget to take a trip to anywhere in the world and with anyone they want to accompany them. Give them ten to fifteen minutes to write out their itinerary – ask them to be specific and as detailed as possible about where they are going, how they are going to get there, who is accompanying them, where they will

DREAM TRIP EXERCISE

Team members write and share a detailed itinerary and plans for an all-expenses paid trip to the location of their choice.

TRUST

> Research has shown that teams need trust to perform well and to become high performing.
>
> Be sure to give trust to gain trust.

stay, and what they will do." ("The Team Building Directory - Dream Trip" 2018)

"When time is up, everyone will take turns sharing their trips for five minutes. In less than an hour of interaction, a lot about the style and personality of each team member will be revealed."

Heda also suggested that Rhett schedule monthly team lunches and other fun events so everyone would get to know each other better. She assigned Rhett do an Internet search for additional team building exercises – that would be his homework for the evening.

She next wanted to talk about management through influence. While it is a critical skill which managers of all levels need to master, it's especially important for project managers as they do not have any direct management authority over the project team.

"At Xanadu, we communicate with WhatsApp and slack," stated Rhett. "I can let the team know when we are going to get together."

"I'm not familiar with those applications," said Heda. "Maybe you could show me how they work?"

As they finished breakfast, Rhett gave Heda a quick overview of the applications and promised to share more detail later.

"Trust building and getting to know each team member personally will help to increase your personal influence on the team." continued Heda when they were ready, "You need to lead by example to succeed."

"For one, you have to include the team in all major decisions that affect them. This will increase their buy-in to any decisions made. While you may not always be able to enact their decision, you should then be transparent and communicate why that could not or did not happen."

Heda further explained that Rhett had to acknowledge the work of the team as a group and as individuals (Umlas 2006). This could include:

- Recognition when key milestones are met, even with just a "thank you"
- Scheduling monthly team lunches or other fun events
- When something extraordinary is accomplished, report it to management in the next status report, being sure to credit those who made the effort
- Anyone who did something extraordinary more than twice in a quarter should be nominated for a quarterly Xanadu management award: a $100 gift certificate for the employee and a guest to have dinner at a nice San Diego restaurant

Showing Rhett by example that he was learning and absorbing the information he needed, as the morning turned to noon, Heda led Rhett down the block further to a small café where they enjoyed a light lunch as they continued their conversation. By the time they moved back to the Xanadu conference room, they were ready for the next topic.

Suddenly, Heda's cell phone rang in her purse and she pulled it out to answer. Rhett was completely surprised as her phone had been silent up until now. She listened carefully for a few minutes, occasionally nodding her head. When finished, she thanked the caller, then hung up.

"Rhett," Heda began, looking more serious than before, "there's been a slight complication with your project. Rick met with the Xanadu resource manager, and the in-house QA team is going to be engaged in other projects at about the time we expected them to test the Clark Inc. application. He's gotten senior management to sign-off on a contract with Pointeast Technologies, a leading IT service company in Manilla."

"Pointeast has a rigorous independent software testing service and an excellent reputation," Heda stated confidently. "As a result, you will not just have to work with the development team in San Diego; you will also have a virtual team in the Philippines. We'll need to spend some time this afternoon preparing to handle a virtual team."

Heda explained that while all communications will be in English, for most of the team, English will be a second language. In addition to all the other points of teams and communications already discussed, Rhett will have to communicate clearly and concisely so as to be understood. He will also have to make sure his messages were received and interpreted as intended. He has to practice active listening, making sure he confirms what he hears in his conversations with them.

While much of the communications may be conducted by email, Rhett will also have to maintain personal contact with the Pointeast project manager and team. Heda recommended the use of Skype or Zoom calls so that he can have face-to-face discussions. Use of these conferencing applications will enable them to obtain clarity and closure more quickly. They can also participate in some meetings with the rest of the team.

"Time will present some issues," Heda stated. "First, daylight savings time is not observed in the Philippines. The country is fifteen hours ahead of San Diego when daylight savings time is observed in California, sixteen hours when it is not. So optimal time for conference calls will tend to be around the end of the work day in San Diego. This will be the start of the next work day in the Philippines. Rhett, you will have to take this into account when scheduling meetings and planning deadlines."

Time zones aren't the only time challenge. Many Western countries, including North America and most of northern Europe tend to see time and deadlines as linear and fixed. Time is perceived as money, so time commitments need to be met is the prevailing work attitude.

Rhett's QA team, however, was from a reactive culture that views time more cyclically. People from reactive cultures spend more time listening and trying things, less time planning. It's more about the journey than arriving at the destination on time. A lot more communication will be required to manage expectations and make sure the QA team stays on track (Lewis 2014; "Reactive | Cross Culture" 2018).

Finally, the distance itself will present challenges such as making it more difficult to build trust, giving a feeling of isolation, having a lack of social interaction, and failing to instill an overall team spirit. Rhett will have to research other cultural differences such as holidays, so they can both celebrate and factor them into plans (Bailey 2013). Heda supplied him with a Virtual Team Contact Template so that he could begin to record some of the important information about differing cultural needs.

Heda advised that if they had good requirements, Rhett could start working with the QA team early so plans could be put in place that would have a high probability of success. Heda was confident that Rhett would be able to handle this new aspect of the project.

"We have one last topic today that we need to discuss," continued Heda, "and it's an important one."

"A big event for the team will be the project kickoff meeting, and you will need to carefully plan for it. This will be a chance for Sally from Clark Inc. to meet the team as the client and Rick will play the role of Xanadu project sponsor."

"Who else should be invited?" Rhett inquired.

"Since some of the team members report to different functional managers, the functional managers should be invited as well so they can see how their resources will be used and what they can do to support the project."

"The team will be together to begin getting acquainted with each other and learning about what the client and project sponsor envision for the project in terms of the high-level scope and approach to the project. If timed right, the project manager from Pointeast could also join via video conference so the team understands there will be remote participation in the not too distant future."

"You should think about the agenda for this meeting – I've got a Kickoff Agenda Template you may consider. You may also want to be sure it is a GREAT meeting as we discussed when looking at meetings for eliciting requirements."

Heda further explained that this is where Rhett should share the high-level Work Breakdown Structure and start assigning team members to look at the various components. The work of creating the WBS should begin the day after the kickoff meeting if possible.

Clarity of the purpose, plan, and initial responsibilities will get the team on the right path and Rhett will be in place leading them. They can build on the momentum and excitement set in motion by the kickoff meeting. The clarity and momentum mean that the team will spend minimal time in the "storming" phase.

As the day came to a close, Heda started another story. "Around fifteen years ago, someone I mentored just like you had a difficult project. His goal was to test, upgrade, and retest 10,000 computer systems."

"He hired a team of ten temporary workers to design and perform the tests. The client signed off on the test plans and the project moved forward. The team was doing really well, when a new change was suddenly demanded by the client. The timeline for the project was going to be cut by three to four months. A new, end-of-year deadline was set in place of the prior deadline of the following spring."

Heda continued to explain that while the team continued testing, the project manager worked out a plan to complete the work on time and deliver the systems to the client. He shared it with the team to get their buy-in. It would require the team to expand to thirty to accommodate all the work. Because the team worked so well together, they were able to help the project manager bring the new team members up to speed.

The team split into three teams of ten: one to do the upgrades, one to test, and the third to do a final inspection, packing, and shipping. One of the original team members took charge of each of the new teams and reported daily to the project manager. If upgrades or testing were falling behind, some of the packing and shipping team would be diverted to help out. The systems were all delivered and the client signed off on the work -- the project was a huge success because of teamwork.

Heda, as usual, summarized their learning for the day:

- J is for Jell with the team
- Teamwork is critical for success
  - Trust is essential to healthy teams
  - Teambuilding activities help the team to jell and develop trust
- Management by influence, not authority
  - Trust and teambuilding build influence
  - Team needs to participate in decision making
  - Acknowledge the work of the team
- Cultural challenges of virtual teams
  - Time: time zones and perceptions of time
  - Language and communications
  - Distance
- Project kickoff meeting
  - Invite sponsor, client, team, and functional managers
  - Have a GREAT meeting
  - Include virtual teams

Even with the addition of the virtual QA team, Rhett remained confident that he could handle the teamwork required. He went home to eat dinner before starting his homework.

Knowledge Nuggets

First and foremost, get to know your team very well. In addition to team building exercises, schedule one-on-one meetings. Consider questions such as:

- Where do you see yourself in five years?
- What knowledge or skills do you think you need to develop to get there?
- Within the scope of our work, what kind of assignments do you believe would help?
- What items should the team work on together?
- What can I do to support your development?

Questions like these will not just help you get to know your team better – your team will see you as a leader that is there to support their success.

In a much less direct way, get to know who the team knows, both inside and outside your organization. Teams with challenging assignments don't always have all the answers. When questions and challenges arise, help your team think about who they might know that could help them find an answer.

PMBOK® Guide reading: Part I, Chapter 9 to learn more about project resource management.

Article: How Different Cultures Understand Time (Lewis 2014)

Book: The Power of Acknowledgement (Umlas 2006)

Website: http://www.ventureteambuilding.co.uk/team-building-activities/ provides a list of more than 60 team building activities and exercises

Chapter Templates: Virtual Team Contact Template, Kickoff Agenda Template

CHAPTER 5

DAY 5: EXECUTE EFFORTLESSLY

On Friday morning, Heda was waiting in Rhett's office for his arrival. On the white board he saw:

- Delegate
- Follow Up
- Give Feedback
- Hold People Accountable

"Did you finish your homework?" Heda inquired.

"I did," Rhett replied enthusiastically. "I have a copy for your review."

Heda took time out to review Rhett's team building exercises and gave him some feedback before they started on project execution.

"E is for Execute. We've talked a lot about planning," Heda began. "If you have the best possible plan in place, execution will take far less effort. New problems with people will emerge and you will need to be prepared to handle them. While the team works on the project, your challenges will shift from planning to making things happen. But you need to let the team do the work."

Heda continued her explanation, "One year a project management class I was teaching at a university had a team of web developers in attendance. They always seemed very down, so one day I asked them what was happening. While they were well paid, their manager made all the decisions and managed their workday to the hour."

"They had no room for creativity, innovation, or even to make simple suggestions. They were being completely and totally micromanaged. There was a total absence of trust - basically their manager thought he knew better than everyone. Three months later at the end of the class, they all quit and the company had to close."

EXECUTION

After having a good plan, soft skills will help achieve the best performance:
- Delegate
- Follow up
- Give feedback
- Hold people accountable

Heda knew that Rhett would face many challenges, especially with the addition of a virtual QA team located in another country. He would not have time to do any architecture, coding, or testing on this project – he had to keep his eye on all the moving parts to make sure the team was performing.

While most of the team assignments will come from planning, many more pieces of work would likely reveal themselves during execution. Rhett had to learn to delegate to team members, rather than try to do it all himself.

Heda explained, "Unfortunately new project managers often lack confidence or fear loss of control, leading to lower levels of delegation. Even more unfortunately, loss of control is what normally happens when project managers fail to delegate and do too much by themselves. They have to resist the 'I can do it better or faster myself' thinking and set up a successful delegation."

Delegation taps into the power of the team to accomplish project activities. It can be a learning experience, boost team confidence, and be a step toward developing a high performing team when done properly. Rhett will achieve more by delegating what others can do, even if they are not up to his level of competence, because he can then focus on planning and managing.

There are four key elements to successful delegation:

1. The right person should be selected for the task and empowered to get the job done
2. What needs to be accomplished and any expectations should be clearly communicated
3. The communication should discuss the "what" but leave the "how" to the team member
4. The person delegating should demonstrate confidence that the team member will successfully complete the assignment

"Based on the level of experience of the team member," Heda pointed out, "you can adjust your expectations. A junior team member with little or no experience of a task should be asked to formulate a plan of action to accomplish the task, then come back to you for approval. Someone very senior may be asked to complete the task and report back when it is done."

During project execution, Rhett will need to literally follow-up on his follow-ups, meeting regularly with the team member. Once again, this may depend on experience level. Junior team members may need a daily follow-up – senior team members weekly. Very urgent tasks may require more frequency.

"The best manager I ever worked with was Nathan," stated Heda, "He walked by everyone's office or cubicle at least once a day to greet them by name. He'd say 'Hi Heda, how are you today? Is everything on track?' and if I responded I was fine, he'd move on to the next office. If I had an issue, he'd sit down and ask me to explain how I was thinking of solving it. Usually these just ended with comments like 'You're on the right track, Heda' and he'd move to the next office."

Follow-up is also important for any tasks with close or important deadlines, especially if the task is shared by multiple team members. It's a common team mistake to think that handoffs of tasks are happening as planned – someone may be out sick or a little delayed in finishing their part of the activity, but the rest of the team may not know it or think about it. These types of hidden assumptions can make otherwise successful projects fail.

Follow-up is required to make sure the most urgent and important activities are being completed as planned. If they are not, corrective action may be required. In some instances, it may be prudent to verify status updates to ensure that work has been completed to required standards.

"Feedback is also critical to execution success," continued Heda. "As a project manager, you will need to give both praise and constructive criticism. In both cases, it's best to remain professional, be direct, and stay with the facts, rather than making the feedback about emotions, subjective feelings, or people."

"Also, try to emphasize the positive aspects. Rather than say 'you never contribute enough ideas to the team', try 'I reviewed the meeting minutes and you haven't contributed any new ideas during our discussions of innovation – what are your thoughts on what the team should be doing?' This will open up a two-way dialog and get to the root cause of any issues faster. It focuses on leading the team member to finding a solution, rather than just offering criticism."

As Heda pointed out on the first day, people need the leader to acknowledge their good work and positive contributions. There needs to be a balance between praise and criticism, with more emphasis on praise. Leaders who only comment on performance when there are issues or problems will quickly lose the trust of the team. And trust is essential for a leader to be able to lead by influence.

"Perhaps the most important thing you will need to do during project execution is to hold people accountable," Heda explained.

"Team members need to be expected to make and meet commitments, perform their job responsibilities, and take responsibility to deliver. This is why you ask them to participate in creating the WBS and provide the estimates – they are choosing the schedule and you are negotiating with them, representing what is needed for the project. Many project managers make the mistake of dictating the schedule."

Heda went to the white board and began to write again:

---

1. Be clear what is needed
2. Follow up on commitment
3. Give quality feedback
4. Coach and mentor

"It looks like these are necessary to hold people accountable. Is that true?", Rhett inquired.

"Being clear about what is needed and following up are the first two of four steps in holding people accountable," answered Heda. "When goals aren't being met and activities aren't completed as planned, the team members need to know. They need quality feedback – the third step."

"The fourth step is coaching and mentoring. You will need to have discussions with those not performing up to expectations. It's critical that they understand what is expected and the consequences for the team and organization if the expectations are not met."

"This is not a form of criticism, but an opportunity to discuss with the team member why they haven't been able to meet their commitments and the support and resources they may need to get back on track."

"Rhett, yesterday I mentioned my mentee who was responsible for the project testing 10,000 computer systems. Once that project moved into execution and the testing and upgrade of the equipment started, delegation, follow-up, feedback, and accountability were key to getting the team to their revised end-of-year goal. Every day ended with a brief meeting between the project manager and the unofficial team leads to review issues. The project manager made sure that any requests for additional resources and tools were quickly reviewed and acted on. The team truly became a high performing team."

"I'm confident I can build a high performing team," stated Rhett, "thanks to your guidance, Heda."

Heda continued, "Rhett, I know you will be able to reach that goal - you've been doing well in absorbing the material. We won't work together over the weekend, so please take some time to reflect on what you've learned. If you have any areas where you want more information, dig into the additional materials I've provided. We'll meet on Monday and Tuesday, and your work on the Clark Inc. project will begin on Wednesday."

Heda wrapped up the day with a summary:

- E is for execute
- Good planning makes execution progress more smoothly
- Delegation is important
    - Select and empower the right person for the task
    - Clearly communicate "what" – let the team member work on "how"
    - Demonstrate confidence that the task can be done
    - Make adjustments for the level of experience of the team member
- Follow up early and often
    - Meet/touch base with team members
    - Urgent tasks need more follow up
    - Don't make hidden assumptions
- Give Frequent Feedback
    - Mix of praise and constructive feedback
    - Keep it professional
    - Emphasize the positive
    - Focus on solutions, not the criticism
- Hold people accountable
    - Be clear what's needed
    - Follow-up on tasks and delegations needs to be early and often
    - Give frequent feedback – praise and criticism
    - Coach and mentor to sustain and improve performance

Rhett left feeling good about what he would be able to accomplish with Heda's help. He would spend some time studying over the weekend to prepare for the project start on Wednesday.

Chapter Pro Tip: Say "no" without saying "no", set limits without setting limits.

The most effective project managers learn to say "no" without actually using the word "no". "No" has an air of finality and disempowers the team.

Try some of these alternatives instead:

- Yes, and in exchange I will need "x". Will that work? (say yes and get something in return)
- I'm worried about "x" now, so would "y" and "z" work instead? (suggest alternatives)
- Given "x", how would you like me to proceed? (point out a downside to "yes" and get input)
- Would you please help me prioritize these actions? (help the priority of a "yes" to be considered)
- May I make an alternative suggestion? (a more direct way to suggest alternatives)

In a similar manner, setting arbitrary limits can be equally challenging. Rather than set a limit on number of issues, for example, find another approach. For example:

- Define multiple categories for issues and clearly define what goes in each "bucket"
- Clearly specify time frames for addressing items in each category
- When there are more issues than you can handle, you can either wait it out or bring in more resources
- If a higher number of issues than expected happens for a prolonged period, you can re-think quality plans and re-define priorities

> Using these techniques will empower team and establish you as a respected and trusted leader.

PMBOK® Guide reading: The PMBOK mentions many skills but does not provide much information about them. Some aspects are covered by Section I, Chapter 4 on project integration management.

Article: Project Manager Accountability (Jordan 2017)

Website: Learn more and test your delegation skills at Mindtools.com ("How Well Do You Delegate? Discover Ways to Achieve More" 2018)

CHAPTER 6

DAY 6: CONTROL CASUALLY

On Monday morning Rhett arrived early, refreshed from the weekend and feeling confident from his review and study. Heda was already waiting for him and once they exchanged pleasantries about their weekends, she was ready to begin.

"C is for control," she started. "With controlling, you set your project parameters, monitor them as the project is in progress, and make some changes as necessary. Controlling is only second in importance to planning. One common mistake that new project managers make is to either under control or over control. Think of it like under steering or over steering a car – neither are likely to get you to your destination safely."

"So, what is the right amount of control?" Rhett inquired.

"The right amount of control is in place when there are no surprises," Heda exclaimed. "A firm and steady guiding hand – disciplined but with a suitable level of informality. Pay more attention to overall trends than one-time small deviations. And have checks and balances in place for your most important constraints such as time and resources. We'll consider how to best accomplish the right level of control today. Do you remember the construction of Petco Park, the baseball stadium in San Diego?"

Rhett nodded – he went to ball games regularly and knew there were some problems before the stadium opened.

"When the construction was about half completed, the entire budget had been spent. How can something like this happen?" Heda asked.

"I see," Rhett mused, "there must have been some inadequate controls in place. Otherwise how could they miss a gap that big?"

"Precisely!" exclaimed Heda. "Without appropriate controls, projects aren't completed as planned and customers are usually unhappy. Let's take a look at the basics to put in place to help avoid these issues."

First Heda explained that once the milestone plan was in place, it would become what is known as a baseline. That baseline would remain untouched, and Heda let Rhett know that either she or Rick would let him know if a change to it is necessary. Every week, Rhett would measure the variance, the number of days the development team deviated from plan.

"Your initial reaction to the first sign of variance will be 'I've got to do something to correct that'," said Heda. "While it is in our nature to want to solve problems, it's important not to overreact. Some activities may be done early, some may be done late. If everything is going smoothly, they will even out over time. On the other hand, if there is a trend – key tasks are late several weeks in a row – you will need to consider how to best correct the issue."

Some of the possibilities for correction include:

- Wait longer – see if the problem corrects itself
- Take an action – for example, ask someone to work overtime or ask someone else to help
- Replan some other work – change some assignments or look for some unimportant work that can be eliminated
- Consult with the project sponsor and client – they will reserve the right to take other actions, such as to cancel or postpone the project

"I have a Project Control Chart Template you can use to plot the project time variance. You know the team and the product well, Rhett, and Rick and I will be here to support your decision-making process. If you take on more responsibilities in the future, the concept of baselines and variance will work for other project plans, such as budgets."

Next, Heda went on to explain that Rhett had to master controlling requests for changes to his project, including the requirements, outputs, and deliverables: the scope of the project.

"Once the requirements are completed and the project starts, the scope of the project, like the milestone plan, should also be considered to be baselined. Invariably someone will want a change to the requirements. The best approach is to consider the change a possible opportunity."

"Capture all the information about the change. Carefully evaluate the change. How will it impact your plan? What resource, risk, and other impacts will it have? Once you analyze the change, present it and the potential impacts to Rick and Sally at Clark Inc. Let Sally make the decision based on the information you provide. And be sure to touch base with Rick as the Xanadu sponsor. You will need to understand from them who has the final right to approval."

"I get it!" exclaimed Rhett. "If the client approves the additional funding, time, or resources, then we can implement the change. If they decide to postpone it to a future date, we still all benefit. Change can be an opportunity for future project work."

NO GOLD-PLATING

Giving a client more than they asked for without a change request is referred to as "gold-plating".

This is common in software projects and can have negative consequences such as exceeded budets and timelines, increasing project risks, and customer backlash.

"Correct," reinforced Heda. "You will also need to be sure that the team knows that changes are not to be made without going through the process. It may be easy for them to do, but blindly accepting changes is not beneficial. Use the Change Request Template I'll provide to capture the information. It will provide a complete record for the change."

"What other things do I need to be concerned about to control the project?" Rhett inquired.

In return, Heda posed a question, "Have you ever heard of Elmer Wheeler? He was at one time considered to be America's top salesman. He is credited with the phrase 'Don't sell the steak, sell the sizzle!'"

"He had two other famous phrases that are applicable as well: 'Don't write – telegraph' and 'Watch your bark'. Each week you will need to provide a status report." As she continued, she wrote on the white board:

Right message, right time, right format, right people.

"Like Elmer, you want to telegraph – keep the messages short and concise. The initial words are most important."

"I've always sent Rick a weekly status report but didn't pay too much attention to what I wrote," responded Rhett. "I've never heard of Elmer Wheeler."

"Elmer's sales tactics are still practiced today. A status report will help you maintain control because it keeps everyone informed about the project progress," continued Heda. "As Elmer would say, you also have to 'watch your bark' – consider the language you use."

"Because you are addressing people at all levels of the organizations involved in the project and may need their help in controlling the project, be sure your messages are short and to the point, and easy to understand. Status reports are also a great opportunity to acknowledge and praise the team for a job well done – 'sell the sizzle'. Be sure to include successes and give credit to those who helped the team achieve them."

Heda continued to explain, "There is a tie-in with status reports and stakeholder analysis. Be sure to understand up front what the right time, the right message, the right format, and the right people are. You may also need to schedule face-to-face meetings with Sally and/or Rick. Your communications should be detailed in the stakeholder register and communications plan which we looked at the first day."

"I'll provide you with a Status Report Template as a starting point but be aware this one may require the most tailoring to be appropriate for your audience," cautioned Heda.

"Now would be a good time to review the stakeholder register and communications plan and make sure these communications are included," continued Heda. "You also need to understand that any identified corrective actions used to set the project back on the right course must be sufficiently gentle so as not to oversteer."

"The best approach is to start by having a direct conversation with the team or team members that are falling behind. Let them know that there is an issue and ask for their help. Most good team members will take the opportunity to offer up suggestions for correction themselves. They may volunteer to put in some extra hours or suggest they can come in on a day off. Let them choose how they will fix the issue. You should discuss with Sally and Rick at what point they want to hear about this information."

"It's also important to minimize the work associated with status reports and meetings. Project controls in excess may themselves derail a project. Each meeting or other control consumes time and resources. So carefully evaluate how you want to expend that time and budget."

"What should I do if a bigger correction is needed?" inquired Rhett.

"If a larger correction is necessary, be sure to involve the team. More heads are better than one," continued Heda.

"Together the team will often find a solution. Empower them to do it. You are there to coach and mentor if they get stuck or cannot find a suitable path. And if you are unable to, Rick and I are here to support you."

"A former client of mine had a great way to conduct a status meeting. They had a project that involved fifty software and hardware engineers. Every Friday there was a one-hour status meeting with all the engineers that always finished on time, if not early – it was an expensive meeting. The project manager went down the long list of tasks for the week and asked if they were all complete, one at a time. If the answer was 'yes', she moved on to the next task. If the answer came back 'no', an appointment was set to discuss the issues later in the day. It was just that simple."

"There were some immediate benefits. Since everyone on the team knew who was ahead and who behind schedule, best case they could offer their assistance and worst case, they could stay out of the way while those who were behind caught up. And since the meeting was kept to an hour, it was an invaluable way to share the information."

"Wouldn't it be a surprise if your client's project manager found out on Friday that work wasn't completed?" inquired Rhett.

"Absolutely," said Heda. "Remember my best manager, Nathan, who walked from office-to-office daily?"

"I do," said Rhett as he suddenly saw the connection. "I'm sure by the end of the week he had a pretty good idea of how the work was progressing. And he had an opportunity during the rest of the week to think about the need for corrective action. But what if a team member isn't forthcoming about an issue?" he inquired.

"By keeping in regular contact with the team, that will be difficult for someone to do. And if it does happen, you just need to be sure that team member knows that they are accountable for their work and their actions, and hiding an issue isn't acceptable," explained Heda. "You need to be sure everyone knows that the best project environment is where there is a lot of open, transparent communication. It's OK to discuss issues and make mistakes. Have them think of mistakes as learning opportunities."

As the Monday drew to a close and the project start date was only two days away, Heda asked Rhett to summarize this time. He included:

- C is for control.
- Develop plans, then baseline them. Measure each week for variance.
- Be sure control is casual – don't oversteer or overreact. You can:
    - Wait a little longer
    - Take a small action
    - Replan some of the work
    - Consult with the project sponsor and client
- Master change control
    - Baseline all requirements and plans
    - View change as an opportunity
    - Capture and analyze the information
    - Let the client and sponsor decide
    - No changes that haven't followed the process
- Regular status reports
    - Short and concise
    - Consider the language used
    - Successes and recognition
- Flexible and Gentle Steering
    - Don't oversteer
    - Control controls – they expend resources
    - Empower team to find solutions

"Good job, Rhett!" Heda exclaimed. "You understand the basics of control. Tomorrow is our last day together before the project begins, so try to relax these next two evenings."

Chapter Pro Tip: Compile useful information as you go.

Projects generate vast amounts of data beyond the normal "lessons learned". As the project progresses, collect, index, and perhaps even diarize this data. It contains information such as:

- Plans and changes to plans
- Performance of the project and people involved
- Value and benefits the project provided
- Problems faced and decisions made
- Value added ideas for the future of the project
- Memorable things people said

This level of historical data may not only help in future projects and learning but may boost your career with valuable ideas and accomplishments you might otherwise forget.

PMBOK® Guide reading: As a process, monitoring and controlling occurs throughout all the knowledge areas. Refer to Table 1-4 for the specific sections.

Templates: Project Control Chart, Change Request, Status Report

CHAPTER 7

DAY 7: TRANSFER

It was now Tuesday morning and the seventh day of his preparation. Rhett knew that tomorrow the project would start, and he felt that Heda had prepared him well. They had one last day together and he was prepared to make the most of it. Heda wasn't in his office, but he found her in the conference room, writing on the board:

Every project is an opportunity to learn, to solve problems, to embrace opportunities, and to transform the team.

"Good morning, Rhett," started Heda as she turned around. "Just as Olympic gymnasts have to 'stick' their landings, project managers need to bring their projects to a successful conclusion and learn from the successes and failures along the way. Today we're going to talk about two T, transfer, to prepare you to 'stick' your project's landing."

"Heda, I'm feeling really prepared and want to thank you for all you've done to help me. I've learned a lot and I'm going to do my best not to disappoint anyone," stated Rhett.

"You're welcome, Rhett," Heda continued. "Getting the project into user and customer hands successfully is what most people will remember the project manager for, so this is very important."

"I worked with a project manager a long time ago that had not learned this lesson. The project was to develop a reporting application for a customer that sold a software service to their customers. The goal was to produce the reports the first day of each month. The application had both development and testing issues, and then was put into production without proper planning."

"What kind of impact did that have?" inquired Rhett.

Heda went on to explain that the reports were delivered on the first of each month, but one full month late. Support personnel were sleeping under their desks to restart the application which would fail frequently and need to be restarted. The team invited Heda to help solve the problem, and she found a simple answer.

Rather than restart from the beginning, the output could be saved and appended to. The fix took six lines of code and came close enough to the first of the month that the developers were able to spend some time to make some other corrections and optimizations to completely meet the goal. With the chaotic transfer of the application, including serious issues, the application was not acceptable to the customer.

"Rhett, when you transfer the product to Clark Inc. to put into production, you need to make sure everything is in order and delivered per the agreed requirements. They need to get the 'white glove, red carpet' treatment – they will feel good not just about the product, but you and your team at Xanadu. This means that:

- The product is fully tested and any known issues are documented, including any workarounds
- There should be a meeting with Sally and her team from Clark Inc. to demonstrate the product and officially turn over its operation
- The demonstration should be based on their acceptance criteria and tests for the project
- Use the meeting ask Sally and her team if there are any other tests they may want to have performed
- Plan to have a full user acceptance test and document the results before the final transfer of the project takes place and it is put into production
- Final requirements and training documentation, user guides, any operational information such as roles, user names, and passwords, and other documentation requested should be ready for Sally and her team and provided at that meeting as well
- You and your team will support Sally and her team as needed for the first few weeks until they are comfortable – after that support will be turned over to the Xanadu support team.
- You consult with Rick to find out if there are any other requirements he or Xanadu has to complete a project."

"At this point, a complete and professional transfer will help to get Sally and her team up to speed and prepare them to sign off on your project."

"I can do that," Rhett added confidently. "I'll make sure that the tasks of our testing, user acceptance testing, and documentation are also included in the milestone plan."

PROJECT MANAGERS AND ETHICS

Project management involves people - people making a lot of decisions, some of which revolve around ethical dilemmas and difficult choices.

Ethics is about doing things right. Ethical decision making, trust, and integrity all contribute to high performing teams and leaders.

"That's how to do it," encouraged Heda. "All the work needs to be in the plan so there are no last-minute scrambles to accomplish work that wasn't in the plan."

"You will also need to measure your delivery. You may recall that WashCo set a performance goal of no more than ten minutes to process the data and display the dashboard. I understand that Clark Inc. has told Rick that they would like to have that reduced to five minutes, so that will most likely be an identified requirement. You should go back to all the requirements which are measurable and make sure the product meets all their goals."

"I'll make sure that also gets into the plan. What should we do, for example, if we are close to the goals but not quite meeting them?" Rhett inquired.

"The best thing to do when something is close is to be honest and transparent with the client. Inform Sally at Clark Inc. as soon as you discover any performance or other limitations. You want to get her feedback in advance, if possible, in case major changes to the requirements, scope, or product need to be made."

"If you are able to get the performance to five and a half minutes instead of five, determine what it will take to get to five and review the results with Rick and Sally. Clark Inc. may agree to accept the dashboard if there is a plan in place to meet the goal shortly after delivery. Or alternatively, if you can demonstrate why it might not be possible, they may also accept it. What you don't want to do is promise five and have them discover it is really six after they accepted the delivery. You should do what both demonstrates integrity and ethics throughout the process."

After Rhett had a few minutes to think about their discussion and jot down a few notes about the closeout planning required, Heda continued. "Rhett, if you establish yourself as having basic management skills, your career at Xanadu will be on the rise. In practice, Rick should evaluate the team. But he won't be working with them on a day-to-day basis like you. As part of the project wrap up you should write short evaluations for each team member."

"I'll provide a Team Member Evaluation Template which will stress both accomplishments and areas for development. I know Rick will appreciate the information. The project manager for the WashCo project you worked on did this – it's how you were identified for this opportunity."

"There is one last item we need to work on – lessons learned", stated Heda. "Rhett, thinking about how we spent our time together over the last seven days, what worked best for your?"

"Well, to start with," Rhett began thoughtfully, "I really liked the way the time was structured. You had stories from real experiences and situations which illustrated the points. Then, we did a deeper dive into the specific areas. And at the end of the day, you always summarized. The variety of meeting locations and some of the 'homework' assignments also helped to make everything more memorable. The PROJECT methodology is going to be very hard to forget based on how it was presented."

"Excellent!" exclaimed Heda pleased that her mentee was doing well and most of all, learning. "What do you think could be improved?" she asked next.

"That's a little harder to answer right now," Rhett said. "Everything seemed to go very well. I just wish there was time for more practice of the concepts. But the templates you are providing will help and I'm willing to put in the extra effort as the project gets underway."

"Outstanding," stated Heda. "I will give consideration to adding more practice to my presentations. I may even document everything in a book so other clients like you will be able to refer back to concepts and review them as the project progresses."

"What we just accomplished, Rhett, is how lessons learned can be completed simply for your project," said Heda as she jotted down on the board:

- Ask what was done well and worth repeating
- Ask what needs improvement for the next time, or perhaps that we shouldn't do any more
- Share with Rick so he can share with the other managers to immediately put plans in place to act on the feedback for the next project
- Use the feedback to improve your delivery of the next project
- Continue to work as necessary to integrate the changes into your routine and that of other Xanadu project managers

---

Too many project managers skip this step, stating a lack of time. But including our discussions, how long did this take?"

Rhett thought for a moment and saw Heda's point: conducting a lessons learned meeting does not have to take a lot of time or create more overhead. In a little less than an hour Rhett provided feedback to Heda and she was prepared to act on it in the future.

"Less than an hour, so it didn't take a lot of time," he stated out loud. "I think this might be a good way to implement continuous improvement in project management."

"Exactly, Rhett," said Heda. "And you don't have to wait until the end of the project. You might work with the team to gather lessons learned after each project phase or after some major deliverables have been completed. I'll provide a Lessons Learned Template which will help to organize the information and remind you of the opportunities to collect it."

"After the failure of the reporting project that I spoke of earlier today, I convinced the project manager and management of the company that they needed to improve a lot of things. Rather than do everything at once, we made a list and prioritized it. With each new project they continued to add and prioritize, as well as implement items on the list."

"I also developed the templates over time for them. Their project manager tailored them for their specific projects. Their next projects were far more successful and they managed to repair the relationship with the client."

So, as she did the previous day, Heda asked Rhett to summarize what they discussed and learned together that day:

- T is for transfer
  - Transfer the project to the client
  - Transform the team through evaluations and lessons learned
- Treat the client with white gloves
  - Transfer fully tested product, including client acceptance test results
  - Meet with client for turnover
  - Provide training and all documentation
  - Provide good support to see the client through the transition
- Measure Your Delivery
  - Meet client requirements and other expectations for performance
  - Measure performance whenever possible
  - If close, facts and negotiation with client may help
  - Demonstrate integrity and ethics for best results
- Team Evaluations
  - Short feedback document
  - Stress accomplishments and development needs
  - Provide to management without any expectations
- Lessons Learned
  - What worked well
  - What needs improvement
  - How will we act on this for the next project(s)?

Before departing for the day, Rhett and Heda spent some time reviewing each of the daily summaries and Heda helped to fill in some gaps. In just seven days, Rhett learned the basics of good project management to succeed. He left feeling confident that he would be ready to start the project the next day.

Chapter Pro Tip: Do the right thing, even when no one asks or is watching.

Ethics is about doing the right things, and when you have integrity, you will continue to do them, even when no one is watching.

Projects can be full of ethical dilemmas – the difficult choices we have to make. These occur in many circumstances in project management, as you and the team are pressured by stakeholders to:

- Produce incomplete reports, half-truths, and lies with statistics
- Skew results "just a little"
- Delay reporting to avoid negative data or emphasize positive data
- Develop scapegoats – who to blame for poor results
- Emphasize one area to avoid another
- Report positive or negative progress not supported by data
- Make unapproved changes or "gold plate" the project
- Not exercise due care – not follow processes

As you are confronted with choices and have tentative solutions and decisions, consider the following questions:

- Am I feeling pressured to decide one way or the other?
- Does the decision meet requirements, is it legal, and is it in conformance with all regulatory requirements and organizational policies?
- Is it fair and balanced for everyone concerned?

> - How will I feel about myself once I go home?
>
> Keep in mind that trust and integrity are essential to team work and maintaining your ability to manage by influence. Once an unethical behavior is uncovered, it is difficult to regain the trust you will need to succeed.

PMBOK® Guide reading: Section 1, Chapter 4.7 covers the project close out process; for more information about ethics, visit: https://www.pmi.org/ethics.

Templates: Team Member Evaluation, Lessons Learned

CHAPTER 8

EPILOGUE

Wednesday morning, Rhett was at Xanadu bright and early. He had a number of appointments already scheduled over the next few days to begin identifying the project stakeholders and finding out about internal expectations for the project before heading to Clark Inc. the next week to begin elicitation of requirements. As he neared the end of elicitation, he sent Rick his suggestions for team members and scheduled the kickoff meeting.

Rhett had copious notes to review, templates to modify and fill out, meetings to schedule and plans to be made after his consultation with Heda. In their short time together, Rhett and Heda actually learned from each other. Rhett was pleased with the result and confident he would be able to manage the project.

As the project progressed, Rhett kept reviewing the PROJECT methodology and using the templates that Heda provided. Rather than just use them as is, he carefully reviewed them and modified them as needed for the project, satisfying both Xanadu's and Clark Inc.'s needs specific to the project. This helped him tremendously as the project would not be without issues. But as promised, Heda and Rick were available as needed to help him clear roadblocks, listen to any issues he had in making decisions, and provide other support as needed.

PROJECT MANAGEMENT CAREERS

Project management careers are built from both learning and experience. Working on both together is a good approach.

As you learn more, consider taking the CAPM® Exam which is a terminology test. It will demonstrate a commitment to your employer.

As your career progresses, in three to six or more years you should be able to sit for and pass the PMP® Exam.

As a result of his preparation, Rhett successfully navigated through some of the more difficult aspects of project management:

- The team did a more thorough job identifying stakeholders, gathering requirements, and organizing and documenting plans
- The team, client, and other stakeholders always knew what had to be done next
- The estimates for the project were the most accurate Xanadu teams had ever made
- Rhett regularly met with team members and provided feedback
- Follow up on key assignments and delegations happened daily as needed
- Rhett provided regular project progress updates to the customer and Xanadu leadership team
- Team members weren't just accountable for their work – they took pride in it
- As he wrote evaluations, Rhett beamed with pride as everyone performed well
- Rhett maintained the visibility of the project which also helped to motivate the team

As the project was well under control, Rhett began studying the many project topics that Heda wasn't able to include in her seven-day preparation, including:

- Schedule network diagrams for project timelines
- Basics of budgeting and finance
- Earned value management systems
- Advanced estimation techniques
- Organizational structures and management theory
- Procurement documents and processes
- Basic tools of quality
- Full treatment of all the processes, including project initiation, full scope, risk, and change management
- Additional soft skills such as negotiation and conflict resolution.

The Clark Inc. project completed in less than a year as the client expected, and was considered a huge success, both by the client and Xanadu.

In between projects, Rhett continued to build his knowledge of project management and more advanced project management tools like Microsoft® Project®. After he completed a few more projects, the company grew and a new management position opened – guess who filled it?

The opening occurred because Rick moved up in the organization. He recognized that it would be difficult for Rhett if he didn't have training and mentors to help him. And the success that he created with that approach helped to earn him a place in senior management.

As for Heda, after a long and successful career as a project manager and an equally long and successful career as a project management consultant, she memorialized the PROJECT methodology in a book and headed to a tropical beach in parts of the world unknown. She was satisfied that through her book, she could help accidental project managers like Rhett to:

- Become heroes in their organizations by succeeding with their projects
- Master the easy basics of project management
- Build credibility as project managers
- Use the advice, tools, and templates to make sound decisions for their projects
- Identify future learning goals and needs
- Start building long term careers

Do you know someone who is or is about to become an accidental project manager? Do them a favor and share Rhett's story with them.

FIN

Author's Notes

The templates referenced in this book (as well as in other PPC Group, LLC publications) are available "as is" for your download, modification, and use. To access them, please visit https://ppcgroup.us and click on *Membership Levels* in the navigation. Sign up for a free "*Platinum*" membership to create an account with access to the resources.

The table at the end of these notes shows the skills incorporated in this book versus the skills covered by or mentioned in the *Guide to the Project Management Body of Knowledge – Sixth Edition*. Although referred to as a "quick start" guide, the material in this book touches directly and indirectly on a substantial number of skills and knowledge areas.

What I hope the reader will understand is that project management is a journey more so than a destination. There is no easy way to absorb all the skills and knowledge required in a term or semester, let alone seven days. By getting started and focusing on basics and building from there, readers will gain a very solid foundation and have plenty of time to learn the more advanced topics not covered in this book. Think of it as your continuous improvement.

Keep in mind that the PMP® Exam requires a minimum of three years of work in project management which gives you plenty of time to study advanced skills like Earned Value and Network Diagrams and look at each of these competencies in more depth.

Primary Competency	Sub-competency	Book Coverage
Know-how	Domain Know-how	*These are the subject matter, industry and organizational specific skills learned on the job and as part of regular career development.*
	Technical Know-how	
	Process Know-how	
	Financial Management Know-How	
Personal Excellence	Negotiation	
	Integrity and Ethics	√
	Respect for individual	Indirect
	Attitude & Perseverance	Indirect
Team / Internal Stakeholders Management	Leadership	√
	Oral Communication	√
	Written Communication	√
	Delegation	√
	Team Management	√
	Networking & Collaboration	Indirect
	Accountability	√
	Managing Conflict	
Thinking Skills	Problem Solving & Decision Making	Indirect
	Analytical Thinking	Indirect
	Innovative/Creative Thinking	
	Questioning/Probing	Indirect
Customer Management	Cross-Cultural Competency	√
	Customer Awareness	Indirect
	Oral Communication	Indirect

		Indirect
	Written Communication	
Project Management Knowledge	Integration Management	√
	Scope Management	√
	Schedule Management	√
	Cost Management	
	Quality Management	
	Resource Management	√
	Communication Management	√
	Risk Management	√
	Procurement Management	
	Stakeholder Management	√
Project Management Processes	Initiating	
	Planning	√
	Executing	√
	Monitoring & Controlling	√
	Closing	√

Table 1: Coverage of Project Management Competencies

References

A Guide to the Project Management Body of Knowledge. 2017. 6th ed. Pennsylvania: Project Management Institute.

Andersen, E. S. 2006. Milestone planning—a different planning approach. Paper presented at PMI® Global Congress 2006—Asia Pacific, Bangkok, Thailand. Newtown Square, PA: Project Management Institute. Available at: https://www.pmi.org/learning/library/milestone-different-planning-approach-7635.

Anderson Economic Group. 2017. *Project management job growth and talent gap 2017-2027*. [ebook] Newtown Square, PA: Project Management Institute, pp.6, 8. Available at: https://www.pmi.org/-/media/pmi/documents/public/pdf/learning/job-growth-report.pdf.

Bailey, Sebastian. 2013. "How to Overcome the Five Major Disadvantages of Virtual Working". *Forbes.Com*. Available at: https://www.forbes.com/sites/sebastianbailey/2013/03/05/how-to-overcome-the-five-major-disadvantages-of-virtual-working/#28aff5d62734.

Baker, E. 2012. Planning effective stakeholder management strategies to do the same thing! Paper presented at PMI® Global Congress 2012—North America, Vancouver, British Columbia, Canada. Newtown Square, PA: Project Management Institute. Available at: https://www.pmi.org/learning/library/planning-effective-stakeholder-management-strategies-development-6058.

Buffett, M. & Clark, D. 2006. *Warren buffet's management secrets*. New York, NY: Scribner.

Crowe, A. 2006. *Alpha Project Managers - What the Top 2% Know that Everyone Else Does Not*. Atlanta, GA: Velociteach Press.

Davis, A. M. & Zweig, A. S. 2000. Requirements management made easy. *PM Network, 14*(12), 61–63. Available at: https://www.pmi.org/learning/library/requirements-management-made-easy-phases-4616.

Forman, J. B. & Discenza, R. 2012. Got stake?: (Holder) management in your project. Paper presented at PMI® Global Congress 2012—North America, Vancouver, British Columbia, Canada. Newtown Square, PA: Project Management Institute. Available at: https://www.pmi.org/learning/library/stakeholder-management-plan-6090.

Frohnhoefer, R. 2007. *Communicate, Communicate, Communicate – Precise Projects Consulting Group Blog.* [online] PPCGroup. US. Available at: http://www.ppcgroup.us/wordpress/2007/09/communicate-communicate-communicate.

Frohnhoefer, R. 2011. *You Know You are a "Knighted" Project Manager When … – Precise Projects Consulting Group Blog.* [online] PPCGroup. US. Available at: http://www.ppcgroup.us/wordpress/2011/01/you-know-you-are-the-knighted-project-manager-when.

Frohnhoefer, R. 2015. *Plan Projects like Albert Einstein! – Precise Projects Consulting Group Blog.* [online] PPCGroup.US. Available at: http://www.ppcgroup.us/wordpress/2015/04/plan-projects-like-albert-einstein.

Frohnhoefer, R. Frohnhoefer, Ray. 2017a. *Risk Assessment Framework.* Escondido: PPC Group, LLC.

Frohnhoefer, R. Frohnhoefer, Ray. 2017b. *Risk Assessment Framework Implementation Guide.* Escondido: PPC Group, LLC.

Haus, Marian. 2016. "Are Your Communication Habits Good Enough?". *Projectmanagement.Com.* Available at:

https://www.projectmanagement.com/blog-post/18979/Are-Your-Communication-Habits-Good-Enough--.

Hossenlopp, R. & Hass, K. 2008. *Unearthing Business Requirements.* Vienna, VA: Management Concepts.

"How Well Do You Delegate? Discover Ways to Achieve More". 2018. *Mindtools.Com.* Available at: https://www.mindtools.com/pages/article/newTMM_60.htm.

Hunsberger, K. 2011. The accidental project manager. *PM Network, 25*(8), 28–33. Available at: https://www.pmi.org/learning/library/accidental-project-manager-necessary-skills-2858.

Jordan, A. 2017. "Project Manager Accountability". *Projectmanagement.Com.* Available at: https://www.projectmanagement.com/articles/406759/Project-Manager-Accountability.

Larson, E. 2014. I still don't have time to manage requirements: My project is later than ever. Paper presented at PMI® Global Congress 2014—North America, Phoenix, AZ. Newtown Square, PA: Project Management Institute.

Lewis, Richard. 2014. "How Different Cultures Understand Time". *Business Insider.* Available at: http://www.businessinsider.com/how-different-cultures-understand-time-2014-5.

"Panama Canal". 2018. *En.Wikipedia.Org.* https://en.wikipedia.org/wiki/Panama_Canal.

"Reactive | Cross Culture". 2018. *Crossculture.Com.* https://www.crossculture.com/about-us/the-model/reactive/.

Reina, D., Reina, M. & Hudnut, D. 2012. Why trust is critical to team success. Research Report. Greensboro, NC: Center for Creative Leaderships. Available at: https://www.ccl.org/wp-content/uploads/2017/05/why-trust-is-critical-team-success-research-report.pdf.

"The Team Building Directory - Dream Trip". 2018. Innovativeteambuilding.Co.Uk. Accessed June 29. http://www.innovativeteambuilding.co.uk/activity/dream-trip/.

Umlas, J. 2006. *The power of acknowledgement.* New York, NY: IIL Publishing.

Index

virtual team contact, 57, 62

WBS dictionary, 40, 50

threat, 44, 46, 47

transfer, 90

transform, 90

V

variance, 74, 81

virtual team, 56, 57, 60

W

waterfall. <*See* predictive>

Wheeler, Elmer, 76, 77

work breakdown structure (WBS), 39, 40, 41, 45, 47, 49, 58, 67

workaround, 45